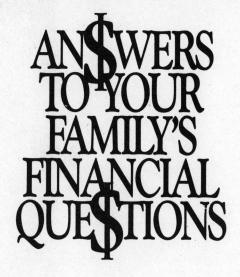

ANSWERS TO YOUR FAMILY'S FINANCIAL QUESTIONS

Larry Burkett

FINANCIAL COUNSELOR

AN$WERS TO YOUR FAMILY'S FINANCIAL QUE$TIONS

PUBLISHING
Pomona, California

ANSWERS TO YOUR FAMILY'S FINANCIAL QUESTIONS
Copyright © 1987 by Focus on the Family

Library of Congress Cataloging-in-Publication Data

Burkett, Larry.
Answers to your family's financial questions.

    1. Finance, Personal.   2. Finance, Personal—Religious aspects—
    Christianity.   I. Title.
HG179.B8349   1987   332.024   87-82303
ISBN 0-8423-0042-2

Published by Focus on the Family Publishing, Pomona, CA 91799.
Distributed by Tyndale House Publishers, Wheaton, Illinois.

Printed in the United States of America

Contents

CHAPTER 1

Attitudes

Money is perhaps the least understood yet most discussed topic in our society. Thousands of families daily make financial decisions based on bad advice.

In reality the only totally reliable advice comes from God's Word. I have found that the Bible addresses virtually every financial decision a person will ever have to make. That's why *Answers to Your Family's Financial Questions* offers advice based on God's Word.

Live question and answer sessions, such as those I do on the radio, are my favorite form of teaching. They provide an opportunity to demonstrate that the Bible is the best source of financial wisdom ever written, and I always try to base my responses around that wisdom.

These sessions also reveal the true attitudes, fears, and frustrations that many people have about finances. They have fundamental questions about real-life problems, but they seldom have a chance to voice them.

For instance, on one program an eighty-three-year-old widow asked if she should mortgage her home and give the money to a financial counselor from her church to invest for her. She needed more income, and he had guaranteed that he could double her money in twelve months. With this she could pay off her home, invest the remaining money, and live off the interest. The counselor probably had the best of motives but the worst of wisdom.

When armed with a few facts, this widow was able to make a decision that probably saved her home. First, I asked her how she would sleep at night if she lost her home. "Not very well," she responded, "it's really all I own in the world."

Then I referred her to Proverbs 14:12, which says that plans that seem right to a man often end in disaster. I also suggested that the counselor put his guarantee in writing.

Later, she wrote to tell me that he refused to do that. Several months afterwards, he filed for bankruptcy protection when the commodity investments he had been selling collapsed.

Many questions that Christians ask are the result of pressures put on them by other Christians. For instance, a Christian wife called in to ask whether she should tithe her salary even if her non-

Christian husband didn't want her to. Several of her friends had said that for her not to tithe would be to deny God.

I shared that God honors the heart attitude of the giver, not the gift itself. Her reward from God was sealed when she made her commitment to give, just as Abraham did with Isaac. In Ephesians 5:22, God's Word says that wives should honor their husbands as they would the Lord. By respecting his wishes, she was removing a potential stumbling block from his path to salvation.

I also suggested that later she go to her husband and ask his permission to tithe from her income and see if they would be better or worse off financially. After all, in Malachi 3:10, God says to "test Me now in this." Such a test would not be conducted for personal gain, I told her, but for God to reveal Himself to her husband.

Nearly two years later, she wrote to tell me that her husband agreed to let her tithe $10 a month. Shortly after that she was made office manager with a net increase in salary of $100 a month.

Then he agreed to allow her to give $20 a month, and shortly afterward he was given a promotion that netted more than $1,000 a month.

Coincidence? Maybe, but he began to go to church with her, found Jesus Christ as his Savior, and now teaches a couple's class on biblical financial principles at their church.

Some of the most difficult financial decisions Christians have to make are those involving children. Because we love them, we want to help them avoid life's pitfalls. But too often we end up weakening their character.

I was counseling a widow whose only daughter, a registered nurse, was forever calling and asking for a loan to help her get by until the next payday. The loans were never repaid, but the mother said she didn't care because she didn't need the money. She and her husband had managed money well, and she had a comfortable income. "What I don't understand," she said, "is why my daughter didn't pick up our habits. We never borrowed money."

I asked her: "Did your parents send you money when you overspent your budget?"

"You have to be kidding!" she replied. "Our parents loved us, but they were farmers and didn't have any money to spare. What we wanted, we worked for."

"Don't you see," I told her, "that you have allowed and even encouraged your daughter to become undisciplined financially? If those habits are not corrected before she gets married, she will end up in great trouble."

I also shared the wisdom of Proverbs 3:12, "For whom the Lord loves He reproves, even as a father [or mother], the son in whom he delights."

She prayed about this counsel and determined that she would not give her daughter any more money. The next time her daughter called, it was to ask for twenty-five dollars for food until the next payday. Her mother asked, "What did you do with your food money, dear?"

"I found a really good buy on a winter coat, Mom," the daughter replied.

"I'm sorry, honey, but I just won't send you any more money. You'll just have to get by on what you have in your apartment and learn to budget your pay."

"But, Mom," she said, "all I have left are some crackers and peanut butter."

"I love you," replied her Mom, "and I know this is the right thing for me to do."

By the time they hung up, both mother and daughter were in tears. Had it not been for the clarity of God's Word, this mother would have mailed a check that afternoon. But she stuck it out. Her daughter survived those two weeks and came out a lot wiser.

Almost ten years later I met the daughter, who was then married with two children, no debts, and a husband who sincerely respects his mother-in-law for her godly counsel.

All these people had real-life questions that not only deeply affected their financial futures, but also their closest relationships. God's wisdom led them to the answers they needed. Real-life questions are asked in this book, too, and God's wisdom serves as the foundation for the answers.

I trust this information will be as much of a blessing in your life as it has been in the lives of others and in mine as I have shared God's answers to families' financial questions over the years.

Question 1:

My wife and I have serious concerns about the affluence in this country. Is it scriptural for Christians to maintain this level of affluence, or should we drastically change our life-styles so we can feed the world's hungry?

God's Word contains an abundance of references about concern for the poor—Psalm 82:1-4, Isaiah 1:17, Matthew 25:34-40, James 1:27, and 1 John 3:17-18—just to mention a few. No doubt our affluence blinds us to the real needs of other people. Many Christians' biggest concern is how to reduce their tax burden, not how to put bread on the table. But to put all this in balance, God's Word does not prohibit a Christian from having a surplus. In fact, I believe that God places Christians at every level of society, from the poorest to the most affluent, so we can witness to those around us.

Psalm 37:4 says, "Delight yourself in the Lord; and He will give you the desires of your heart." What are the desires of our hearts? For those who seek to serve God, it's not material indulgence.

God promises His people an "abundance" if they care about others' needs. "It is well with the man who is gracious and lends" (Ps. 112:5). God has no difficulty with our affluence, provided that it's used to help others and glorify Him.

Question 2:

We have a controversy going on in our church. Our pastor believes that, if you have any problems in your life, it is an evidence of sin. I'm concerned with this philosophy. Eventually nobody will admit to any problems for fear that others will think he or she is sinning. Can Christians have financial problems that are not sin-related?

A current attitude among some Christians is that we should never have problems. If we do, we are being punished by God. What a defeating philosophy!

In James 1:2, God says, "Consider it all joy, my brethren, when you encounter various trials; knowing that the testing of your faith produces endurance. And let endurance have its perfect result, that you may be perfect and complete, lacking in nothing." If you paraphrase that verse, it says, "If you really want to have your faith perfected, you need a problem to test it." Therefore, we know with certainty that problems are not *the* evidence of sin.

Obviously, problems can be an indicator of sin, but there will also be many other indicators, including the sin itself. Christ promises that if we yield our rights to God, we will have peace when (not if) we have problems (ref. John 15:19-20). The Lord Himself had plenty of problems during His time on earth, and if we follow in His steps, we also will have problems. Through our difficulties, we are to be witnesses to others who are having similar problems. By observing us, they will know that our God is real.

One final point: The last thing someone having a serious problem needs is another Christian asking if he or she has confessed all known sins. Most of the people I counsel have confessed every sin at least twice and several they had never done, just to be sure.

Question 3:

I'm discouraged over my financial situation. It seems as though everyone I grew up with is doing well but me. I vacillate between wanting to be content and the fear of being a failure. If God really promises us peace and prosperity, why am I so discouraged?

Why do Christians despair and get discouraged? One reason is because we have adjusted our expectations to the level of those around us. We're not thankful for what we do have; we're depressed over what we might have, but don't.

Most of us suffer from unrealistic expectations of what God has promised. Much, if not most, discouragement has finances at its root. Since many Christians believe that financial success is a testimony to the Lord, failure to achieve success must represent spiritual failure. If a man can't give his family as much as others, discouragement begins to set in.

The key to overcoming discouragement is contentment. Paul said in 1 Timothy 6:6 that ". . . godliness . . . is a means of great gain, when accompanied by contentment." Hebrews 13:5 says, "Let your way of life be free from the love of money, being content with what you have; for He Himself has said, 'I will never desert you, nor will I ever forsake you.' "

Question 4:

I find that as I get older, I worry more about the future. I'm worried about how I could earn a living if I lost my job and what will happen if I can't afford to retire. It seems like I'm paralyzed by fear of the future. I know it's wrong, but how can I change?

Worry has been described as taking on responsibility that belongs to God, and that includes being preoccupied with the future. The Lord said, "Do not be anxious, then, saying, 'What shall we eat?' or, 'What shall we drink?' or, 'With what shall we clothe ourselves?' For your heavenly Father knows that you need all these things" (Matt. 6:31-32). Worry is not the problem; it's an outside indicator of an inside spiritual problem.

Most of our worries are based on future possible problems, not current circumstances. It's the "what if's" that cause us the most grief. Most people can handle the current situation, even a bad one, but they go into depression when they think about the future.

How can you handle worry? Stop, confess that you have assumed God's responsibility, and turn that area of your life over to the Lord.

Question 5:

As a Christian businessman, I make many contracts with people who simply don't keep their word. My question is: Do I have to keep my end of the bargain if the other party reneges?

It's an indictment of our generation that most people (Christians included) don't understand what a vow is. A vow is a pledge to keep our word, literally our honor. Once a Christian makes a vow, it's a binding contract, and must be fulfilled regardless of the cost. Therefore, don't agree to a contract (a vow) unless you understand the total agreement.

You can make a unilateral vow, which means you promise to do something, regardless of what the other party does. Or you can make a bilateral vow in which you promise to do something if the other person does his or her part. You need to be sure that you understand exactly what the guidelines are in a contract you agree to.

Vows seem to be conditional today. Many people feel that a contract made under one set of circumstances can be broken if the circumstances change.

In past generations, vows were a commitment of honor. When an honorable person shook hands, it was a deal. Even if it required all that he owned, an honest man would fulfill his vow. God's Word says, "A good name is to be more desired than great riches, favor is better than silver and gold" (Prov. 22:1). The outside indicator of an honorable person is a good name. I would encourage you to keep your word, regardless of what others do.

Question 6:

I've done a lot of business with people who call themselves Christians. Some of them don't pay their bills; others simply lie about an agreement they made. Do you believe someone can be a Christian and cheat or steal?

Over the years, I have counseled people that I knew to be Christians, who had committed some serious sins, including cheating, lying, stealing. However, if somebody has truly surrendered his or her life to the Lord, that person cannot continue living those kinds of sins for a long period of time. Ultimately, he or she will repent and try to make restitution.

Anyone can sin if the temptation is big enough and he or she isn't prepared to face it. The only way to avoid dishonesty is to predetermine your response to any temptation before it occurs. For example, decide that you're going to pay your income taxes, regardless of the sacrifices necessary. Vow that you're not going to cheat on an expense account, no matter how much you need the money.

Christians must be willing to handle the things of this world according to God's truth. If you're one of those who have stumbled, stop and confess to those you offended, ask their forgiveness, and make restitution (see Matt. 5:23-24).

Question 7:

Could you define what an indulgence really is? I own a Mercedes automobile and a home that's probably worth $200,000, but my income is sufficient to buy both of them, just as easily as somebody else would buy a Chevrolet and a $50,000 home. Are these indulgences because of their cost, even though they hold their value better than lesser-priced items?

God clearly desires that we prosper and that we enjoy the fruits of our labor. However, in the United States I believe that we've stretched this principle beyond the boundaries of common sense. We need bigger and better indulgences to keep us content.

An indulgence can be defined as anything we buy that has little or no utility to us. To determine if something is an indulgence, we have to look into our lives and say, "Am I missing something as a result of not having this? Does this thing enhance my spiritual life, my family life, or my business life?" The cost of the item is not the key factor. Let me give an example.

I have a friend who bought an airplane in the mid-1980s for approximately $12 million. But for him it was not an indulgence.

Why? Because he owned a commuter airline, and the airplane was simply a tool to earn a living. So it had utility.

Utility is relative to our life-styles. For instance, what may be a need in my life could be an indulgence in yours. I have need of an automobile, as most Americans do, but an automobile is a tremendous indulgence for most people in India. Because it's an indulgence for them, does that mean it is for me? Not necessarily. However, even a need can grow into an indulgence.

For example, let's say I need an automobile. But my need can be satisfied with a ten-year-old Chevrolet. My want might be for a new Oldsmobile, and my desire might be for a turbo-diesel Mercedes.

Is a Mercedes an indulgence? It depends on God's plan for your life. Does this mean that a Christian can never live above the need level? Absolutely not. But each indulgence leads to a greater one. Most of us never outgrow the indulgence temptation, but we can learn to control it.

One common symptom of Christians who develop an indulgent life-style is that they are attracted to the prosperity teachers. These teachers proclaim a popular social gospel. They use cute quotes like, "Live like a King's kid," and "Go ahead and do it. You owe it to yourself." Don't fall for that nonsense, or you may end up losing out on the greater rewards. "For everyone who exalts himself shall be humbled, and he who humbles himself shall be exalted" (Luke 14:11).

CHAPTER 2

Husband's and Wife's Responsibilities

Question 1: *Is it scriptural for a Christian wife to work outside the home?*

Question 2: *Must I work if my husband says so?*

Question 3: *Should mothers of young children work?*

Question 4: *What does it mean for the husband to be the authority in the home?*

Question 5: *What if a wife is a better manager than her husband?*

Question 6: *Who should manage the books in the home?*

Question 7: *Should a wife be involved in a husband's business?*

Question 8: *Should a wife be the boss in business?*

Question 9: *What about a wife working in a business in which there are multiple partners?*

Question 10: *Are premarital agreements appropriate in a Christian marriage?*

Question 11: *How can I protect my wife's inheritance if I die and she remarries?*

Question 12: *Should a wife turn over all assets to an irresponsible husband?*

Typically, money is either the best area of communication in a marriage or the worst. For most couples, it's the worst. The pressures of finances on a young couple, especially debts, can destroy a relationship. One partner fears debt and desires to live within the budget but sees the other as uncooperative and indulgent. One may be seen as a "spendthrift," the other as "cheap." Frequently, they square off.

What few people grasp is that spouses are almost always opposites. One sleeps late, the other is "a morning person." One is neat, the other messy. One gets lost, the other follows directions well. One is a good bookkeeper, the other never keeps records, etc. Thus, only if they work together will they be able to fulfill God's plans for their family. "For this cause a man shall leave his father and his mother, and shall cleave to his wife; and the two shall become one flesh" (Gen. 2:24).

Question 1:

I'm a Christian wife and mother who works outside the home. I enjoy my job, and I enjoy my home. But many friends have hinted that I am sinning because I'm not home full-time. Does the Bible teach that wives shouldn't work outside the home?

I don't believe that God's Word teaches that a wife cannot work outside the home, but I do believe it establishes some priorities. First, if a wife is working because a family "needs" the money, it's the wrong motive. Until a couple learns to get along on what the husband makes, there will never be enough. Second, if a wife is working to fulfill her ego, this is also the wrong motive and will often lead to divided loyalties between the job and home.

Proverbs 31 describes the "excellent" wife. Verses 16 and 24 describe her business ventures as well as her household duties. She is described as a working wife and mother who is able to keep her priorities in balance. I believe it is the "balance" that determines whether or not a woman should work.

Paul states in Titus 2:5 that women should be workers at home, subject to their own husbands. Since women are described elsewhere in Scripture as holding down jobs outside the home, I don't believe Paul is giving new counsel. He is simply stating that women should not neglect their family responsibilities by absorbing themselves in outside work, or even church activities.

The priorities for a working wife are:

1. Her husband's approval (Eph. 5:22). (This doesn't mean that she nags him until he agrees.)

2. Her children are well cared for (Prov. 31:27). (Some children are ready for outside training at six, some at sixty.)

3. She maintains her home well (Prov. 31:15).

4. She can balance dual authority at home and on the job (James 1:8—not double-minded).

Question 2:

I really want to be home with my children, but my husband wants me to work because he feels we need the money. I'm almost afraid not to work because we're barely getting by.

Many women with pre-school-age children are working for virtually nothing. By the time you calculate transportation, clothes, child care, eating out, etc., it takes a net income of about $10,000 a year just to break even.

If a husband insists that his wife work, she should clearly state her objection; then she should respect his authority and do as he asks. However, if the decision to have the wife work is motivated by the desire to maintain a certain life-style, then within a year, the couple will find themselves dissatisfied with their life-style once again. The real issue is to learn to be content with your present life-style. "Not that I speak from want; for I have learned to be content in whatever circumstances I am" (Phil. 4:11).

Question 3:

Do you think it is biblical for mothers of young children to work outside the home?

No biblical references prohibit a wife from working outside the home, provided the other areas of family life are in balance. However, just because the Bible doesn't discourage it, that doesn't automatically imply the Bible encourages it. That decision has to be made by each couple.

Also, I firmly believe that most mothers of young children need to be at home. This obviously means that a family has to learn to get along on the husband's salary. During a child's first five years, basic attitudes are developed, and a mother's influence is the greatest. A secular day-care center in particular may mold character in ways that are not Christian. Mothers of older children know that once those early years are lost, they can never be recovered. Many mothers would later trade a hundred times what they earned to be able to have a greater influence on their teenagers.

Also, a working mother may actually spend more than she makes if she has to pay for day care, transportation, and a work wardrobe, not to mention the taxes on her income. Alternatives exist for women whose families need money: selling homemade crafts, telephone survey work, part-time temporary work, babysitting other children in the home, etc.

Question 4:

My husband acts more like a dictator than a leader. He manages all our finances, and I have no say. He buys the food, pays the bills, and even selects my clothes. I want to be a good wife and I know the Bible says my husband is the authority, but shouldn't I have input too?

God directs a husband to give his family balanced, godly leadership. A husband who desires to be a godly leader should take Christ as his example. A gentle leader, Christ never crushed others' spirits to assert His authority. A marriage between two people is much like the relationship between a person's right and left hands: they are well-matched opposites.

The key to a good partnership is to determine each spouse's assets and liabilities and to work together. It helps to remember that "authority" doesn't mean "ruler"; it means "the one who is responsible." Being a good authority means being a strong enough leader not to be threatened by someone else's strengths, particularly the wife's. There is nothing better that a husband can do for his children than to unconditionally love his wife. The Bible tells husbands to love their wives and treat them as partners (co-heirs) so that God will listen to them (1 Peter 3:7). Acting as a dictator is a sign of insecurity.

In Ephesians 5:24, Paul says that just as the church is to be subject to Christ, so also the wife ought to be subject to her husband. However, the wife is not a "non-person" in the home. She is a helpmate. One of her responsibilities is to help her husband make decisions. Proverbs 12:15 says, "The way of a fool is right in his own eyes, but a wise man is he who listens to counsel." The most trusted counselor any man has should be his wife.

My counsel is: Share with your husband how you feel and offer some alternatives. He may not even know how important it is to you to be involved in making decisions.

If, after sharing your feelings, your husband is unresponsive, I would suggest you both seek a counselor. With this third party involved, both you and your husband can share how you feel.

If your husband is unwilling to go to a counselor, write him a letter, telling him how you feel and offering some reasonable alternatives to the present situation. You could say something like this: "I feel God has created me to be your helpmate. I would like to help by handling the budget for the household items." Try to find some common ground to agree on.

Question 5:

I find that I am a better leader in our home than my husband is. If I don't intervene, my husband allows our kids to come and go as they want, leave our cars without gas, leave their rooms a mess, and on and on. He is their "buddy." I end up being the "ogre." He will never question a price or challenge a salesman. I

called around, checking home insurance costs, and reduced our
payment by one-third. My husband wouldn't do it because the
agent is a friend from church. Don't you think God can assign the
leadership of a home to a woman?

God has assigned that role to the husband. A godly wife must
support him and yield her rights to him. Sarai, in Genesis 12, respected her husband even in his time of weakness and compromise.
She saw Abram's potential, even as God did, and yielded her
rights.

A wife desires strength in her husband, tempered by gentleness.
Your husband does show gentleness; he needs help to develop
strength. I would advise you not to gossip or complain about him
to others. Encourage him. Be the absolute best friend he has ever
had. Allow God to use your wisdom, but leave the results to God.

A Christian wife is to be a helpmate to her husband. That requires good, honest counsel, and then allowing him to make the
ultimate decision. This is the perfect picture of our relationship to
Jesus Christ.

Question 6:

I keep the home financial records because I have more time
than my husband. But I heard a Christian teacher say that the fi-
nancial records are the husband's responsibility. What do you
think?

As I stated before, God usually puts opposites together. If a
wife has the ability to manage home finances, there is nothing unscriptural about her doing so. Both husband and wife should develop their financial plans together, however, so that she is not required to make all the decisions. If there are financial problems,
especially delinquent bills, the husband should take charge and
work out arrangements with creditors. As the authority in the
home, he should bear the emotional pressures of creditor harass-
ment. "Husbands, love your wives, just as Christ also loved the

church and gave Himself up for her" (Eph. 5:25). In the final analysis, if you're the better bookkeeper, keep the books.

Question 7:

Should a wife be involved in her husband's business?

God establishes a husband and wife as a team. This relationship is not limited only to the home. A husband who does not involve his wife in business decisions has lost the best counselor available to him.

The argument is often given that the wife doesn't understand the business. Well, neither did most husbands when they began. Learning is a process, not a revelation.

How involved a wife can or should be day-to-day will depend on many factors such as skill, desire, children, etc. But how involved she can be in business policy is a matter of choice.

I know that I depend on my wife Judy's judgment when it comes to evaluating people and their motives. She has very good discernment. When she became involved daily in the ministry, I found it was best for her to have specific responsibilities, so she is in charge of our conference center. Obviously, she also helps me make policy decisions affecting the ministry.

Question 8:

I started a small business out of our home several years ago. It has now grown into full-time work, and my husband would like to quit his job to help me. Since it's a business that sells primarily to and through women, they will always look to me as the "boss." Is it scriptural for my husband to work for me?

The Bible gives guidelines, or at least references, to wives in positions of authority. One of the most familiar is that of Deborah, wife of Lappidoth, who was judge over Israel (Judg. 4). Clearly, it's difficult for a wife to lead and still honor her husband. Some couples manage in these circumstances very well, but most do not.

Genesis 2:24 defines the marriage relationship as a husband and wife becoming "one person." A couple need to ask themselves if they can fulfill that definition while working together. But the issue for many couples is not the relationship; it's image. In our society, image can be all-important. If you, as a wife, can honor and respect your husband while you are the authority in your business, then you are closer to being "one person" than many couples ever will be. My advice is to forget about the image and do as God leads you.

Question 9:

My husband is a doctor, and I'm a trained office manager. He would like me to manage his office, but his partners resent any family involvement. Are we wrong to want me to be involved?

I suspect you now know why partnerships are so difficult, even among Christians. There are legitimate reasons why some companies don't allow family members to work together. Normally, they want to avoid nepotism (granting special privileges to family). In your situation, I rather suspect it's a case of, "If I can't do it, nobody else can." Or one or more of the partners doesn't want his wife involved. Rather than say that, the doctors may have simply established a policy covering all family members.

If you and your husband believe God wants you to work as a team, it may well mean you will have to withdraw from the partnership. No matter what, you must do what you believe God desires for you. "Better is a little with the fear of the Lord, than great treasure and turmoil with it" (Prov. 15:16).

Question 10:

I have a sizeable trust fund from my parents. I'm engaged to be married, and my mother says we should have a prenuptial agreement specifying that my assets would not be a part of our common estate should I die first or should we ever divorce. My fiancé doesn't care. What should I do?

Such an agreement will eventually drive a wedge between you and your husband. It presupposes that the marriage will not survive; it's really a plan for dissolution. In no sense of the word can such arrangements be viewed as a wife honoring her husband (or vice versa).

Proverbs offers great wisdom to any Christian woman contemplating such a move: "The wise woman builds her house, but the foolish tears it down with her own hands" (Prov. 14:1). It would be far better to refuse the trust than to risk the marriage for something as trivial as money.

I once had a counselee tell me, "I always have a prenuptial agreement so that if I make a mistake in a marriage I won't be penniless."

She was working on her sixth marriage at that time. I believe she was creating the very situation she was trying to avoid.

Question 11:

I am concerned that if I die, someone will come along and trick my wife out of the insurance money. I want to leave it in trust for her so the income can be spent but not the principal. Do you see anything wrong with this?

Basically, there is nothing wrong with leaving your assets in trust for your wife. In many instances, this is a good financial planning tool.

A caution, however. If you are committing these assets, including the income, to a trust which can be used only for your widow, then I believe it is unscriptural.

If your wife remarries, she is bound to her new husband, and they are to be one. Whatever assets she has should also be available to him. If they are to be one, there can be no barrier between them. You would be doing her a grave disservice if you tied up the income from the trust so that it could never be used for their common benefit. I would refer you to what the apostle Paul said in Ephesians 5:22: "Wives, be subject to your own husbands, as to the Lord." You don't want to be guilty of interceding in that relationship.

Question 12:

My husband seems to have suffered a deep emotional trauma and is now acting irrationally. He spends money on a whim and buys boats, cars, condominiums, etc. This is out of character for him, and it frightens me. As co-owner of our business, I have been hiding money in the company so that I can pay the bills and our employees. Am I wrong to do this?

This situation is not unique. Many men go through mid-life crises, and I assume this is the situation. Quite often a man in his late forties or fifties will go through a personality change and act irrationally. It's usually temporary.

Encourage your husband to seek professional help to ensure it's not something more serious, such as a chemical imbalance in the body or a psychological dysfunction. I suggest that you not turn over all the finances to your husband while he is in this irresponsible stage. You have a responsibility as a wife and co-owner of the business to ensure that the bills and payrolls are met.

There are instances in Scripture in which the wife had to assume responsibility because of the husband's irresponsibility. When Nabal was acting foolishly before David, Nabal's wife Abigail intervened to keep David from attacking him. She was blessed for her action while Nabal was punished for his irresponsibility.

Proverbs 12:4 says, "An excellent wife is the crown of her husband, but she who shames him is as rottenness in his bones." I encourage you to execute your duties in a quiet and confidential manner so as not to bring shame to your husband, either from the employees or the creditors.

Question 13:

My husband and I are committed Christians. Over our lifetimes we have accumulated a sizeable estate. It is our desire to begin disbursing our assets to our children, but after hearing one of your radio programs dealing with a wife being separated from her husband as the result of her finances, we wonder whether we should leave an inheritance to our daughter. If we do, should it be left in trust for her, and if so, what should be the conditions of the trust?

Clearly there is nothing scripturally wrong with leaving assets to your daughter. An inheritance was common to Jewish tradition and to God's Word. Typically, a daughter would inherit property only if the family had no sons. When she married, she would pass the property along to her own sons.

If you are going to leave an inheritance to your daughter, I suggest you: 1) Consider carefully how much to leave her and why you want to give it to her. 2) Not establish the trust so that the funds can never be administered by your daughter and her husband together.

I have counseled couples in which the wife had assets that were kept from her husband (voluntarily or involuntarily) by a parent. With few exceptions, it created tensions in the marriage, particularly when the husband felt his wife was independent of him. I encourage you not to allow that to happen to your daughter.

Question 14:

I am a remarried widow. My husband and I are in our late sixties. Should we keep his assets separated for his children and my assets separated for my children?

One nice thing about God's Word is that it is clear and concise regardless what our age, assets, or opinions. Once you are married, you and your husband are one. If you totally agree to keep the assets in trust for your individual children, that's fine. But if you can't agree on what to do, then spend time praying and seeking God's plan. Even though you are in your sixties, God still has given the leadership in the home to the husband, and the wife is to honor her husband as he is to love her—principles we have heard so often. I trust that after you pray, you will be in agreement about the distribution of your assets. If you can't agree, I encourage you to seek a counselor in your area to help you work this out. Above all, don't let this become a conflict in your marriage.

Question 15:

We are parents of a daughter who is engaged. We want her and her husband to enter marriage knowing how to handle money. How do we teach them God's principles?

Almost fifty percent of the marriages in the United States end in divorce, and the vast majority of those couples say the primary reason is financial problems. If you want to help your children have secure marriages, then make sure they know how to handle money properly.

They should see a trained financial counselor if possible. If none is available, then have them develop a budget for the first year that includes their total income and spending plan. Next, have them demonstrate that they both know how to balance a checkbook. Third, discuss the uses of credit and have them promise in writing not to use credit except for budgeted expenses that can be paid off every month. Last, have them agree to meet with you at least once a month for the first year to review their budget. By doing these things, you will provide them with good financial counsel. As Proverbs 19:20 says, "Listen to counsel and accept discipline, that you may be wise the rest of your days."

Question 16:

My fiancé and I are wondering how much money we should save before we get married. He feels that we should have at least ten thousand dollars, and yet I can see that it would take us several years to save that amount. Can you give us some guidelines?

Every couple getting married should have some savings. At

minimum, it should be enough to pay for the honeymoon and the incidental expenses they will incur during the first two to three months of their marriage, until they settle down into a routine. The actual amount that each couple need will vary depending on the circumstances. For instance, if both are working and need cars, clothes, and all the expenses associated with setting up housekeeping, then their need for savings is going to be much larger than a young couple in college living in a low-cost apartment and being supplemented by their parents. I would say, in general, that any young couple should have one thousand dollars or more after all wedding and honeymoon expenses have been paid.

Keep in mind the principle taught in Proverbs 21:20, "There is precious treasure and oil in the dwelling of the wise, but a foolish man swallows it up." Save in anticipation of marriage, knowing that you will incur incidental expenses. Without savings, quite often a young couple will end up in debt, using their credit cards for what they consider to be necessary expenses.

Obviously, many couples get married without a savings account and still make it, but let me caution you that others get married without any savings and quickly find themselves in debt. The probability of having a successful marriage, especially during the first year, goes up greatly if you have enough savings to handle unexpected contingencies.

Question 17:

My fiancée and I come out of very different financial backgrounds. I am from a family of modest income from the Midwest, and she is from a very affluent home, with a father who is a professional. His annual income is the equivalent of ten years of my father's income. Do you believe these differences are great enough that we should not get married?

Different financial backgrounds can have an enormous impact on a marriage, but different backgrounds do not dictate a marriage's failure. Interestingly, it isn't always the spouse from a wealthy background that is the spender while the spouse from a poor background is the saver. Quite often the opposite is true. If the money in the wealthy home was managed wisely, that partner becomes a prudent money handler. But the one from the poorer family may feel as though he or she did without at home and now is going to enjoy life. In great part, success depends on background, training, and personality.

You both need to discuss this area honestly before marriage. If you find you cannot agree, you probably need to postpone your marriage. Many couples think that simply because they are Christians they can work it out later. Let me assure you that Christians also get divorced over money problems. Proverbs 22:3 says, "The prudent sees the evil and hides himself, but the naive go on, and are punished for it."

Question 18:

My fiancé is in grad school, and we plan to marry next year. I'm wondering if it's proper for a wife to be the primary wage earner while her husband goes to school. Is this taking authority away from the husband?

You need to discuss this issue with total honesty. Ask yourself the following questions: Are you willing to work? Do you want to? Does it bother you that your husband is not working? What would happen if you wanted to go back to school but couldn't while he was in school? What if you got pregnant?

I can see nothing wrong with a wife working while the husband is in school, but no matter what, a husband should also work to provide income for his family. As Paul said in 1 Timothy 5:8, "But if anyone does not provide for his own, and especially for those of his household, he has denied the faith, and is worse than an unbeliever."

There are grave dangers for a young couple when the wife immediately goes to work to support the husband. The first is the wife's resentment if she doesn't want to work, and the second is the husband's feeling of inadequacy.

I have known many couples in which the wives worked, and the marriages were fine. But I have also known others in which the marriages dissolved because of the conflicts this caused.

Question 19:

I'm engaged to a Christian girl from a fine family, but she is simply unwilling to discuss finances. This is important for us because I believe God has called me to the mission field, and I know that I'm not going to make much money. I want to know exactly how she feels about this, but her parents never talked about money and neither will she. Her father handled everything, and her mother never knew how much he made or where it went. What should I do?

You should delay your marriage until you and your fiancée can discuss your finances and your career. Initially, many young couples say, "God will just provide for us." That is true, but I am also mindful of Proverbs 16:9: "The mind of a man plans his way, but the Lord directs his steps." We are to be part of God's plan, not observers of it. If you marry with these uncertainties about your wife's feelings, you may find out too late that she resents your career path and the tight money that accompanies it. Let me assure you that it does not get easier once you are married; it gets significantly more difficult.

Question 20:

My fiancée and I are getting married soon, and we have a question about whether we should rent an apartment or try to buy a home. We get a lot of conflicting advice. My parents have told us that it's foolish to waste money on rent and get no return at all. However, most of the homes we looked at are beyond our financial capability. My fiancée's father is willing to lend us the down payment and even to help make the monthly payments for the first year. Is this wise?

The decision about buying or renting depends on your budget only. If you have the money to make a down payment and you can afford the monthly payments, it's probably wiser to purchase. However, in the case you presented, someone is lending you the down payment, and you would be taking on monthly payments larger than you can afford. That's called a "contingent liability." Scripturally what you're doing is called "surety," and you're taking a risk that can cause you great grief.

I appreciate the concern of your parents in thinking that there is no gain in paying rent when you can be accumulating equity. But let me assure you that you can accumulate debts quicker than you can accumulate equity. The number-one cause of financial difficulty for young couples is purchasing a home more expensive than they can afford. You say your father-in-law will make the monthly payments for the first year. What happens after the first year, when you have to make them?

Bear in mind Proverbs 24:27: "Prepare your work outside, and make it ready for yourself in the field; afterwards, then, build your house." In your case, this means secure the salary that you know will pay for the home and then buy or build one.

Question 21:

Our daughter is engaged to a young man who is going to be a juvenile counselor. He will not be making a great deal of money, but we can help them purchase a home and a car and can supplement their monthly budget. My wife thinks we should do this, but I sense this might not be wise.

God's Word says that when a man gets married, he should leave his father and mother and cleave to his wife. By supplementing this couple's monthly budget, you could encourage them to be dependent on you rather than each other. It's a great idea to help them with a home, but consider waiting until after their first year of marriage, when things are more settled. There is nothing wrong with helping a young couple get into a home, if you are careful not to usurp the husband's authority over his wife, even though she happens to be your daughter. Helping newlyweds with a car is an excellent idea. It should be made clear, though, that the car is theirs, not hers. You don't want your daughter to use the car as a threat during an argument.

I caution you about supplementing their budget every month, unless there are unique circumstances. You could easily encourage them to live beyond their means. God can provide for them just as He has for you. Allow them the opportunity to trust Him in their finances.

CHAPTER 3

Budgeting

A budget is nothing more than a short-range plan for how you will spend your money during the coming year. A budget should not restrict your freedom to enjoy life; it should expand it. "How," you say, "can living on a budget expand my freedom?" By helping you live within your means and not go into debt. If you're already in debt, a budget will help you out of it. A budget is not magical, and living on one won't permit you to spend more than you make and avoid debt. But a budget will tell you when you have spent all you can afford to each month in each category, such as entertainment, food, and gasoline. A budget also tells you how much you must save each month for one-time annual expenses, such as car insurance, property taxes, and clothing.

The simplest budget system is a series of envelopes, one for each category of spending. All you do is write on each envelope the amount to be allocated from each paycheck, and put that amount of money in each envelope. The key to making this system work is not to rob one envelope to feed another. If you do, the money won't be there when you need it, and you'll eventually have to borrow.

Obviously, most people today use checking accounts, and a budget can work equally well with one. Instead of envelopes, an account sheet is used for each category of expense. When you spend, subtract the amount from the appropriate account sheet. Thus the account sheets determine your spending, not how much is in your checking account. A surplus in checking does not represent a windfall profit. It's budgeted money that has not yet been spent.

Question 1:

My husband thinks we need a budget, but I don't see the purpose. I manage money rather well and don't spend more than we make, and I think a budget will be too restrictive. However, I want to be open to the Lord. Are there scriptural reasons to budget?

The purpose of budgeting is to free you, not confine you. God expects us to be a participant in planning a budget, not an observer. As Proverbs 16:9 says, "The mind of man plans his way, but the Lord directs his steps." Therefore, as we apply practical concepts in handling our money, God provides godly wisdom. It should free you from worrying about whether the annual insurance payment will be made, whether you put money aside for the taxes on your home, and whether enough money will be available to buy the clothes your children need. If those are not problems for you, you're among the fortunate few. They are problems for the majority of Americans, and they may well be problems for your children when they have families. If you're not willing to live on a budget, you will not be able to help them live on budgets. So a budget can be a good teaching tool, as well as a good measure of self-discipline.

Scriptural guidelines for budgeting can be found throughout God's Word. For instance, Proverbs 27:23 says, "Know well the condition of your flocks, and pay attention to your herds." If you don't happen to have any herds and flocks, God is probably saying, "Know well the condition of your clothing budget, your housing budget, and your food budget."

Furthermore, a budget can be used to develop good communication between husband and wife. It's one of those issues you can sit down together to discuss, and then come to a reasonable compromise. A budget is really very simple. You have a given amount of money to spend. A budget helps you decide how you're going to spend it.

Question 2:

My wife and I tried to start a budget once, but we got discouraged because we never seemed to have enough money in each category to make the budget work. We were constantly borrowing from one account to help out another. How do we get started and how do we make it stick?

The first step is to know how much money is available each month and where it's presently being spent. Write down exactly how much money comes in from every source. That includes salary, bonuses, gifts, even income tax refunds. That total for the year, divided by twelve, becomes the monthly budget.

Step two is to determine how much you spend and where. A good way to do this is to look back through your checkbook for the last twelve months and divide your expenses into categories: tithe, taxes, housing, automobile, food, etc.

However, many people write checks for multiple categories. In other words, you might write a check for two hundred dollars in the grocery store, and yet only one hundred dollars of it was actually spent on groceries. If this is the case in your family, both husband and wife should keep spending diaries for a month or two. Everything that you spend during this period must be logged into your diary, divided into categories.

Then compare your diaries and draw up a composite picture of what you're actually spending. Some expenses will be non-routine, such as clothing, annual insurance premiums, and car repairs. Average these expenses to make your monthly budget realistic. (For example, if your diary shows that you are likely to spend sixty dollars in three months on clothing, you will need to set aside twenty dollars a month for this purpose.)

Step three is to draw up a realistic budget for the next twelve months. Set aside one day for both of you to prepare your budget.

The sum of all categories in your budget should amount to no more than one hundred percent of your income. Here are estimates for what average families spend in each budget category:

1. Housing—32 percent. This includes everything associated with the home, such as payments, taxes, repairs, and utilities.

2. Food—15 percent. Remember that everything you buy in a grocery store may not be food. Some expenses should be charged to other categories.

3. Automobile—15 percent. This includes payments, license plates, repairs, gasoline, insurance, etc.

4. Insurance—5 percent. This includes all insurance not paid by your employer, such as life insurance, disability, etc. For a fam-

ily not covered by group insurance, this amount will be closer to 10 percent.

5. Debt—5 percent. This includes payments on credit cards, miscellaneous loans, etc. It does not include house or car payments, which have their own categories.

6. Entertainment and recreation—7 percent. Eating out, vacations, soccer, and Little League fit into this category. Obviously, this is one of those categories that must be diligently controlled if your budget is to work.

7. Clothing—5 percent.

8. Savings—5 percent. This is miscellaneous savings for things that you simply cannot anticipate.

9. Miscellaneous—6 percent. This is the category that often eats up all of your surplus, and you can never remember where it went. It includes things such as cleaning, cosmetics, haircuts, cash in your pocket, lunch money, etc.

Now comes the most important step: to live within the budget! It requires discipline on the part of both the husband and wife. Remember what Proverbs says: "A little sleep, a little slumber, a little folding of the hands to rest, then your poverty will come as a robber, and your want like an armed man" (24:33-34).

Question 3:

My husband and I started to budget several months ago, but it has been a point of anger and strife. It seems that whatever we do, we do to the extreme. My husband is so committed to this budget that he allows no flexibility whatsoever. We have eliminated all entertainment and recreation, all new clothing, and have sold my car. He now is seriously considering selling our home and moving into a much smaller home, even though our budget is balancing fine. Can you help?

Genesis 2:24 says God created a husband and a wife to be one. That means that a budget must work for two people and not just for one. A common error in budgeting is to try to overcorrect previous bad habits. Crash budgets may work on paper, but not where people are involved.

I saw this principle demonstrated in one of the first couples I ever counseled. The husband was a financial analyst with a Harvard MBA, but he didn't know how to balance his own checkbook. After our second counseling session, I asked them to go home and develop a budget to control their miscellaneous overspending. (Miscellaneous is that category that eats up your money, and you can never remember where it went.) In their case, they were overspending approximately five hundred dollars per month on a variety of things.

They left and came back in about two months. I asked the husband, "Well, how do you like the plan so far?"

He said, "This is great! I've got our spending under control, and we're not going any further into debt. In fact, we're actually paying off some of our indebtedness and have a small savings."

I asked his wife, "How do you like the plan so far?"

She said, "This is absolutely the worst thing that has ever happened in my life."

"Why is that?"

"I thought you told me this would be a plan that would work for both of us."

"That's right."

"Well, let me tell you something. He has decided that my hair is miscellaneous, our kids are miscellaneous, my car is miscellaneous, the house is miscellaneous. . ." She went on to name the things that he had trimmed out of the budget.

"But," she said, "his bass boat is not miscellaneous. When the motor on his bass boat broke and he had to spend two hundred dollars on it, it was a necessity of life."

Obviously, he had made out a budget that worked very well for him, cutting his wife's discretionary spending, but sacrificing none of his own.

I shared a reference in Proverbs that I thought would fit the situation perfectly. "The way of a fool is right in his own eyes, but a wise man is he who listens to counsel" (12:15). The primary counselor of any husband is his wife.

Question 4:

I am a salesman, and my income fluctuates from month to month. In fact, some months I receive practically no income at all. How can a budget help me?

Families with variable incomes need budgets even more than families on fixed salaries. Many people on variable incomes get trapped into debt because they borrow during lean months and spend what they make during high income months rather than repay what they borrowed. I might add that not only do salesmen fall into this trap but also professional athletes on extremely high incomes. The typical professional football player's income begins in June and continues through December. If he doesn't budget his money, by January it's generally gone.

To properly budget a variable income, you must determine what your average annual income is. Divide that by twelve, and then develop your budget around that amount. You should put all your income into a savings account and draw your average monthly salary from that, thus averaging out the months of high and low income. I would also point you back to the principle found in Proverbs 27:12: "A prudent man sees evil and hides himself, the naive proceed and pay the penalty."

Question 5:

Whenever I develop a budget, I find there's not enough money to pay all of our indebtedness, plus current living expenses. We're seriously considering going bankrupt, but I don't believe that's God's will. Can you give us some direction?

Without being judgmental, let me say that I believe bankruptcy is not an option for Christians. Psalm 37:21 says, "The wicked borrows and does not pay back, but the righteous is gracious and gives." If, after developing your budget, you find that you don't have enough money to go around, you must make some critical decisions. First, determine if your budget is indulgent. In other words, month to month, do you spend more than you make? If so, you must cut back on spending, no matter what.

If your primary problem is overspending on consumables, such as food, gas, clothing, vacations, etc., these have to be brought under control or no plan will succeed, not even bankruptcy. You must develop a budget that is as non-indulgent as possible. Once you know exactly what you need to live on, determine how much money is left over to pay creditors. Divide it proportionally among your creditors, and write each of them a letter asking them to work with you. Include a copy of your budget and a chart of creditors. Explain that you're unable to pay what you promised, but you will pay according to your budget. As you have any additional income—from the sale of your home, cars or motor home; from salary increases, bonuses, etc.—use this to help retire your debts.

The vast majority of creditors I have dealt with on behalf of couples would far rather have something than nothing. The only reason that most creditors get angry or nasty is because those who borrowed money don't pay and avoid the creditors rather than being honest.

A word of caution is necessary here. Any time there has been overspending and there doesn't seem to be enough income, it will take six to nine months before your budget balances on a month-to-month basis. Obviously you didn't get into debt in three months, and you're not going to get out in three months. It will take several months to develop the routine of living within your budget. Your resolve will be tested by everything from car failure to washing machine breakdowns.

Don't quit simply because it doesn't work in the first few months. Stay with it. But I don't want to mislead you. It's a lot of fun to get into debt; it isn't nearly as much fun to get out. It requires discipline. But once you commit yourself to doing what is right, don't look back, stick it out. Once you have totally surren-

dered your finances to God and you're willing to obey His principles, God will be faithful and just to forgive you and also to provide what you need on a month-to-month basis. He promises to
meet your needs, and you can claim that promise. But first, you
have to trust Him.

Question 6:

*We're a newly married couple, and we're hoping to start our
marriage on a sound basis. What hidden pitfalls can we expect as
we begin to develop and work on a budget?*

There are several common errors that couples make. Here are
some to watch out for:

1. Don't go to extremes. Some couples become legalistic and
try to control their spending right down to the nickel. Unfortunately, many times it's the husband or the wife trying to control
the other's spending.

The other extreme is that people don't maintain the discipline
necessary to stay on their budgets. Many couples have told me,
"We don't want to think about it. It's too depressing." Let me assure you, to think about how you're spending your money before
you have problems is not nearly as depressing as to think about it
afterwards, when you're trying to climb out of a deep financial
hole.

2. Beware of the "more-money-in, more-money-out" syndrome.
This means you spend more simply because you have more. This is
particularly dangerous if the extra money is temporary income or
income generated by the wife, which could be stopped by preg-
nancy, getting laid off, husband getting a job transfer, or a variety
of other things. I suggest that you not include the wife's income in
your monthly budget. Save her money and use it for one-time purchases such as a car, down payment on a home, or vacations.

3. Don't think "a little debt won't hurt." Generally, the "little
debts" come from taking a "needed" vacation that is more expensive than you can afford. Or it comes from gifts that you just had
to buy; a car you had to have; etc.

A little debt will hurt, because once you've developed a cycle of debt, it grows and grows. Eventually you find yourself borrowing money just to make payments on the money you borrowed. So limit your debt right from the start.

4. Avoid the use of automatic overdrafts of your checking account. An automatic overdraft allows you to write a check for more than you have in your account, which becomes a loan from the bank. I have counseled couples who ran up thousands of dollars in debt on overdrafts before they realized it. This does two things: It encourages you to be lazy and not keep good records, and it builds debt that is difficult to reduce.

5. Avoid automatic tellers, with rare exception. Many people fail to log automatic-teller withdrawals in their checkbooks, and they end up writing bad checks. Also, it's easy to develop the habit of using the cash withdrawal to buffer your budget when you have spent what you originally allocated.

6. Balance your checkbook. You need to make an absolute commitment to do this monthly, down to the penny. It's not difficult to do, and any bank has a convenient form, showing you how to do it.

7. Be aware that perhaps the most common budget error is simple discouragement. Remember, if your budget doesn't work the first month you try it, developing a realistic budget takes time. Habits change slowly, especially spending habits. It may take six months or more before your budget begins to work well. At times your resolve will be tested by everything from a clogged sewer line to a broken arm.

But stick with it, and remember, once you have entrusted your finances to God's principles, He will be faithful to provide for your needs. An operating budget is a sign you want to employ God's wisdom in your finances. As Proverbs 24:3 says, "By wisdom a house is built, and by understanding it is established."

Question 7:

We've been on a budget for several months now, but invariably we have a problem when an unexpected expense takes away money that we allocated elsewhere. How do we handle these unexpected expenses?

There are very few unexpected expenses. If you look at your budget on an annual basis, you will find the same unexpected expenses reoccur: automobiles break down, clothing wears out, teeth have holes in them, children are injured and require medical care, etc. A workable budget must plan for these variables.

For example, if you spend $1,200 a year on clothing for your family, then $100 a month must be set aside for clothes. In the months you don't spend that money, it's not a windfall. It's an expense that didn't come due that month; the surplus must be saved for future use. At the end of the month, transfer it into a savings account.

In any given month there may be unused money in a category. If you spend it on other things, your budget will never work. Budgeting is a process of sacrificing short-term spending to accomplish long-term goals.

Question 8:

Your budget only allocates fifteen percent for food, but food costs my family twenty-five percent. How can we reduce this category?

The budget percentages that I use are only guidelines. They represent the average of hundreds of families that I have counseled. If you require more for food, make sure the additional percentage comes from another category and not from credit.

Also, think about ways to reduce food costs. One is to make out menus for the month. From your menus, make out your shopping list. Some women will respond, "Oh, no, I can't do that. It would take two hundred menus." No, it wouldn't. The average family is going to eat between seventeen and twenty-five different meals a month. Your menus are your plan, and it produces your shopping list. When you shop, buy only what is on your list.

Some other ways to reduce a food budget: 1) Never go to the store hungry. 2) Never take your husband to the store (we love junk food). 3) Never take small children with you because most of the junk food is within their reach. 4) Join a food co-op. This is an arrangement in which a group of families get together and buy large quantities at bulk discounts. 5) Clip discount coupons.

I know a Christian lady in the New England area who feeds a family of eight on approximately one hundred dollars a month. You say, "Impossible!" No, it isn't, but it is a lot of work. There are many ways to save money, but most of them will require effort and time.

Question 9:

We have committed ourselves to getting our finances under control, but my worst habit is impulse buying. Every time I go through a store I end up buying something because it makes me feel better. How can I stop this?

In reality, impulse buying is really another form of get-rich-quick. Proverbs 21:5 says, "The plans of the diligent lead surely to advantage, but everyone who is hasty comes surely to poverty."

Here are ideas to help control impulse buying that have worked for many: 1) Never buy anything unless you have budgeted for it or wait a minimum of ten days after you see it. 2) Get at least three prices for the same item from different sources. 3) Maintain an impulse list. Write down what it is that you want, get at least two additional prices, and wait at least ten days to buy it. Never have more than one item on your list. I use this system, and with rare exception, I never buy anything on impluse. Do you know why? Because long before I have found two prices on the first item, I find two more items I would rather have. When I violate my system, and I have from time to time, I end up buying on impulse.

A person could easily go broke saving money on good buys. But the only way to conquer the impulse is self-discipline. Without discipline, no budget will help. "For by what a man is overcome, by this he is enslaved" (2 Peter 2:19b).

Question 10:

I'm trying to put my family on a budget, but I can't see how I can ever afford gifts for Christmas, birthdays, etc. Could you give me some help?

Gifts should be in the miscellaneous expenses category. About the only way that you're going to be able to control those kinds of expenses is to budget for them and stick to your budget.

Let's assume, for instance, that you find you can afford approximately $100 a month, or $1,200 a year, for all gifts. That sounds like a lot of money until you go shopping. It can be spent very quickly, especially around Christmastime. You must discipline yourself not to spend more than you budgeted. That means for most relatives you're probably going to have to send cards.

There are many ways to save money on gifts. If you save your budgeted money from month to month, you can take advantage of off-season sales. For instance, my wife was shopping in a store that was going out of business. They had a close-out sale on pickle and relish dishes with silver handles. She bought several and has used them as wedding and anniversary gifts. As long as you have the money budgeted, you can buy when you find a good deal.

You must, however, discipline yourself to spend only what you allocate. I will guarantee you that as Christmas or anniversaries approach, you will feel guilty because you can't buy your wife or children what everybody else is buying. What will help is to realize that most of them probably have gone overboard with credit card spending and will soon regret it. As Proverbs 13:18a says, "Poverty and shame will come to him who neglects discipline."

Question 11:

My wife and I find ourselves deeply in debt because of a busi-

*ness loss. We are unable to pay the obligations that we have, and
we are going deeper into debt every month. We have a home that's
worth approximately $80,000, and we have nearly $50,000 worth
of equity in it. Would it be beneficial for us to sell the home and
use the money to liquidate our debt of about $40,000, or would we
be better off remaining in our home?*

Quite often a couple in debt has assets that can be liquidated
and applied to the indebtedness. Usually that's the right plan, but
it's not the right first step.

The first step is to determine what caused the indebtedness and
correct it. A normal tendency is to sell an asset, reduce the debt,
and then go right back to business as usual, in which case it's a
full circle.

In your case, since the indebtedness was caused by a business
loss, most probably it would not repeat itself. But by the same to-
ken, my recommendation would be to live on a budget for approximately three months to ensure that you've established the discipline
of managing money before you sell an asset like your home.

The second question that should be asked by any couple contemplating such action is, "By selling our home, will we be able to
reduce or eliminate indebtedness enough to enable us to meet our
monthly obligations, assuming we had to rent or buy another
home?"

In your case, since the debt is only $40,000 and your equity is
approximately $50,000, you obviously would be able to liquidate
your debt. However, since I don't know precisely what the payments are on your present home and what they would be on your
next home, you must consider that.

Question 12:

*My husband and I have been discussing the purchase of a new
car. He says we would be better off leasing the automobile, since
we don't have to put any money down on it and we can pay it off
over approximately the same time period. I don't understand how a*

company could lease us a car with no down payment, and it wouldn't cost us any more than if we bought the car and financed it through a local bank. Could you help us with that?

For a great many families, a new car is beyond the budget. New cars are not only very expensive, but they also depreciate rapidly. As soon as you drive it off the lot, you have a used car with a new-car mortgage on it. I recommend to the majority of couples I counsel that they purchase a good used car (between two and three years old). Obviously, that would eliminate the possibility of leasing, since no companies, to my knowledge, will lease used automobiles.

Many couples who are leasing today do so primarily because they don't have the money for the down payment, and it's the most convenient way to get a new car. Usually they haven't considered all the costs (Luke 14:28).

It does cost more to lease a car than to purchase one over the same period of time. You'll normally pay the leasing company the total price of the car plus their profit. At the end of the lease period, you will still owe a percentage on the car, usually about ten percent. So you don't avoid the costs, you just string them out over a longer period of time. In my opinion, leasing an automobile is not a good deal for a family which cannot amortize the cost as a business expense.

Question 13:

We live on a very limited budget, but we would like to be able to take a vacation. Since the budget will not allow us to do so, it's been more than five years since we've gotten away as a family. Do you have any ideas on reducing vacation costs?

For any irregular expense, like a vacation, you need to budget month by month. Decide on an amount that will fit your budget and discipline yourself to put the money aside. If, for instance, the vacation is to cost $600 a year, then $50 a month must be saved.

Then you must be certain to take a vacation that fits your $600 budget.

You can reduce vacation costs by taking a camping vacation. You can rent a pop-up camper or tent relatively inexpensively, or you might find a Christian friend who owns the equipment and will lend it to you without cost.

One family I counseled said that in the summers they did volunteer mission work in exchange for free lodging. During one summer they volunteered with a church near Orlando, Florida, in exchange for a week's lodging at a church member's home. In fact, the church provided them with tickets to some local attractions.

I believe that vacations (sabbaticals) are a part of God's plan for us as Christians. Pray about your needs, husband and wife together, and allow God to show Himself strong on your behalf. "And my God shall supply all your needs according to His riches in glory in Christ Jesus" (Phil. 4:19).

CHAPTER 4

Money and Children

Question 17: *How do we tell our parents we don't want their money?*

Question 18: *How do I teach a rebellious child about money?*

Question 19: *Should we buy our married daughter a house if we can afford to?*

Question 20: *Should I interfere if my children aren't financially wise with their own children?*

Question 21: *Should I bring my children into my business?*

Perhaps nothing reflects the failure to teach family finances in our society more than the national divorce rate. About half of all marriages fail during the first six years. The average income of divorcing couples is nearly $20,000, so income is not the problem. Ignorance is the problem. Ignorance leads to debt, and debt to divorce.

The average twenty-eight-year-old couple owes nearly $94,000, including a home loan. It's a case of too much, too soon. Young couples simply don't know how to make the right financial decisions for their income. It's the responsibility of parents to teach their children God's principles, and that includes principles of managing money.

When armed with God's truth, our children will be able to detect the lies that society throws at them, lies such as, "Go ahead and do it, you owe it to yourself"; "You need to stretch yourself financially if you're ever to be a success"; and "Interest is a good tax shelter."

Question 1:

How old should my child be before I begin training him to handle money?

The younger the better. In the very early ages (one to six), teach your children through fair but consistent financial discipline around the home. Have some jobs the children do without pay, such as cleaning their rooms and picking up their toys.

As they grow, establish some elective jobs they can do for pay. This might include cleaning the garage, washing cars, and mowing lawns (yours as well as neighbors', when they can handle that responsibility), cleaning the bathrooms, vacuuming, etc. This teaches both the value of money and the ethics of doing a job well. The earlier you begin to do this, the better off your children will be.

Two principles should guide you as you begin to teach your children about finances. First, whatever you do, be fair. Don't overpay, but don't underpay.

Second, be consistent. If you have announced that you won't

pay until a job is done to your satisfaction, then stick to it. If you have promised to pay on completion, pay promptly. Don't promise what you can't or won't do.

One way to teach young children the value of money is to help them establish a goal. This can be as simple as earning fifty cents to buy ice cream, or to save enough to buy a coloring book or a record. Associating work with reward is an important concept. As Proverbs 16:26a says, "A worker's appetite works for him . . . ."

Question 2:

Should a child have an allowance?

Proverbs 3:12 says, "For whom the Lord loves He reproves, even as a father the son in whom he delights." Don't teach your children to expect allowances, teach them to work and earn money. The term "allowance" implies something is given rather than earned. If God doesn't provide us with an allowance, and He doesn't, then we probably should not provide allowances to our children.

If you have a child who demonstrates discipline in handling money and you want to give him or her a gift from time to time, there's nothing wrong with that. Just be certain that you're establishing long-term values in your children that will guide them when they are adults.

Question 3:

How soon should my children begin to tithe?

First of all, you should avoid the "nickel in the plate" syndrome. When the collection plate comes around, don't scramble to find your child a nickel to drop in. This teaches nothing about giving. Children learn about tithing by giving of their own resources. I would suggest that a child tithe as soon as he or she has resources from which to tithe.

At the earlier ages, you're probably going to have to encourage, even insist, that a child give a portion to the Lord's work. At older ages, thirteen, fourteen, or fifteen, depending on the child, you should begin to allow him or her to make decisions about giving.

Remember that giving is nothing more than an outside indicator of what's going on inside spiritually. If a teenager doesn't want to give, don't force it. Try to deal with the real issue.

To make giving real to your children, get them involved in others' lives. If necessary, have their tithes go directly to the support of needy families. Your children will begin to see the direct effect of their giving in others' lives.

We did this early on with our children, and there's nothing more rewarding than seeing a child receive a warm letter from someone he or she has helped financially. This permits a child to see that giving is one of God's ways of participating in someone else's life.

Question 4:

At what age should children open savings accounts?

Encourage your children to do this at the earliest possible age. But help them understand that a bank is not a place where they put money and never see it again. It's a place where money is saved for future use. Young children especially should be encouraged to save for short-term projects, such as a trip, a toy, a tricycle, etc. This lets them associate saving with a reward. I encourage you to add to or match their money. This "bonus" may be the key to start them saving regularly.

Saving money is a short-term sacrifice to achieve a long-term goal. As children get older, help them to begin saving for longer-term goals: clothing; an automobile; and eventually, college.

Saving money is good discipline. As Proverbs 21:20 says, "The wise man saves for the future, but the foolish man spends whatever he gets" (Living Bible).

Question 5:

How can a mother teach her children the value of money if their father spends it foolishly and spoils them continually with gifts? Won't the children learn to imitate the parent who is the least disciplined?

Yes, sometimes children will imitate the least-disciplined parent because children are enthralled with spending, particularly when they are younger. Many times, however, children migrate toward the disciplined parent, because that person represents security. A permissive parent or grandparent could lose the children's respect if he or she gives too freely.

You and your husband should sit down together and discuss this, clearly and objectively, from God's Word. Help him understand that love doesn't mean giving children all they desire. Scripture says that a person whom God loves, He disciplines, and the same is true of parents. A parent who really loves a child will establish boundaries for giving, not to restrict the child's freedom, but to teach the concept of stewardship.

If you're unable to talk about this with your husband, I would suggest writing him a letter about how you feel. Base it on God's principles of discipline found in Proverbs 13:1, 15:5, 19:18. You might also seek out a professional counselor who could help both of you understand the balance between giving too much or too little. Remember, too, that God rarely puts similar people together. One will tend to be more of a giver, and one more of a saver. Working together, you can reach a better balance than either of you individually.

Question 6:

I was listening to one of your tapes in which you said that you loaned money to one of your sons and charged him interest on it. I have two questions that perhaps you can help me with: 1) Do you think it's a good idea for parents to lend money to their children?

2) If your children are Christian, how can you justify charging them interest?

Those are very good questions. First, the reason I loaned money to my son was that I felt certain he would eventually borrow money and would quite probably end up in financial difficulty.

If you lend your children money, lend it only for very specific projects, preferably for things that will help them generate income, such as a mower for lawn-mowing jobs, materials for a car wash, a bicycle for a paper route, etc.

Prepare a written contract, have them read it, explain it to them, and have them sign it. I encourage you to charge them interest, not to make money (in fact, you can return the interest at some point), but to teach them the discipline of repaying a debt.

If you're not willing to enforce the contract, then don't lend the money. Proverbs says, "How blessed is the man who finds wisdom, and the man who gains understanding" (3:13). If you won't enforce the terms of your agreement, you're teaching bad habits. You may be instilling an attitude of indifference toward debt that will haunt your children when they are adults.

Question 7:

As my teenagers grow toward independence, they will be deluged with offers of credit cards. I'm concerned that they will get trapped by easy credit. What can I do now to prevent that?

You can teach your older children how to handle credit cards by letting them use the cards while they are still home. I know many people will be shocked to read this and say, "Do you mean Larry Burkett recommends that children have credit cards?" I sure do. I don't think there's anything inherently wrong with credit cards. It's the way they're used that creates problems.

If you allow your children, sixteen or older, to have credit cards, establish firm rules and enforce them. First, don't let them use their cards for anything that is not in their budget. (So they must have a budget before a credit card.) Second, they must pay off the charges every month, no matter what. Third, the first time they can't pay off their credit cards in one month, you will destroy the cards, and they will not be allowed to have new ones.

If these rules are explained in advance and then enforced, your children are unlikely to have credit card problems as adults. Proverbs 22:6 says, "Train up a child in the way he should go, even when he is old he will not depart from it." Establish fair rules, enforce them consistently, and be firm.

Question 8:

We are middle-class parents, fairly well off. How much should we allow our older children to know about our own budget and about how much we earn as a family? Won't this be overwhelming to them and give them a false impression that we are rich?

I believe it's best for parents to be totally honest with their children. If it embarrasses you to share with your children how much you make and how you spend it, perhaps you're not spending it properly. If you're living under God's system of discipline and managing your money properly, then by all means, let them know.

Also tell your children that they may not be able to make as much when they are working, and therefore they won't be able to manage their money in the same way. Share with them how you spend God's money, including how much you give, how much you pay in income tax, and how much you allocate for every category of your budget. You'll find that your children will develop a much more realistic attitude about expenses. As Proverbs 16:16a says, "How much better it is to get wisdom than gold!"

Question 9:

I want to encourage my children to work, but I don't want to overemphasize the financial reward, and therefore help to develop a greedy attitude in them. At what age do you think children should start to work?

First, please understand your children should get paid for their work. But you need to pay them what the job is worth and not overpay or underpay.

How soon should a child be taught to work? Personally, I believe it should start at about one-year-old. Begin by teaching your children the discipline of cleaning up after themselves and doing specific tasks. At one year, that's probably picking up their toys. As they mature, the jobs you give them, both paid and unpaid, can get progressively more complicated. These include cleaning the garage, washing the car, mowing the lawn, etc. Eventually, they should be allowed to work outside the family; perhaps at a fast-food store, garage, or retail store.

Don't overemphasize the money, but don't underemphasize it either. God emphasizes money in His Word as a means to test our commitment to Him. How your children use their money will provide a good insight into their spiritual commitment. "He who is faithful in a very little thing is faithful also in much; and he who is unrighteous in a very little thing is unrighteous also in much" (Luke 16:10).

Question 10:

Do you think it's a good idea for children to work their way through college, or to pay at least part of their own college costs?

Since all children are different, the same advice can't apply to everyone. But in principle, I believe children should work, not only while they are in college, but also in high school, at least during the summers. Many students go to college only because their parents are footing the bill. If these students had to work to pay tuition, most would probably drop out, and many should.

I worked my way through college, and I don't regret the experience at all. I found that I appreciated my education, and I was still keeping up with other students. On graduating, I had many job opportunities, simply because of my work experience.

Proverbs 16:26a says, "A worker's appetite works for him." If your children are helping to earn at least part of their own way, their education will almost always be more important to them. Although many of them may not appreciate it initially, they'll look back on it with a special sense of accomplishment.

Each family must decide what's best for it. Once husband and wife decide together, share the decision with your children. Give them plenty of time to financially prepare for their college education.

Question 11:

Once our children are grown and have moved away from home, isn't it too late to begin teaching them financial principles?

I can answer this question unequivocally. Never, never, never is it too late to begin teaching your children about finances, particularly God's principles of handling money. In fact, it's often easier to teach those who have made some mistakes. If you find that your grown children are having financial difficulties and are asking you for help, use this as an opportunity to help them get good counsel.

An old—but true—cliche goes like this: "If you give a man a fish you can feed him for a day. If you teach him to fish, you can feed him for life." At a minimum, your financial help should be contingent on them establishing a workable budget and seeking good counsel to help implement it.

Question 12:

We have a grown child who is very slothful. He has managed his own money so poorly that often he doesn't have money for groceries. We don't want to give him any more money, because we want him to learn self-discipline. But he goes to our church, and I find now that he has asked the church for help. When the church helps our son, won't the effect of our discipline be wasted?

This is not as unusual a problem as you might think. Stick to what God has told you to do. Many parents attempt to financially buffer their children, but that usually makes the problem worse, as Proverbs 22:15 indicates: "Foolishness is bound up in the heart of a child; the rod of discipline will remove it far from him."

I encourage you not to worry about the church helping, because ultimately it will learn what you already have concluded—that handouts don't solve the problem. You will only alienate your son if you ask the church not to help him. Tell your son you love him, but that you realize that more money won't help him change his ways, which is what he must do. Let him know you will gladly help him when he is willing to live a more disciplined life.

Question 13:

We have grown children living at home who refuse to take our advice. One can't hold down a job. He refuses to contribute to the family financially. I believe that, as a parent, I have the responsibility to ask him to leave, but my wife can't stand to do that. What should we do?

Weakness is not a substitute for love. As Dr. James Dobson says in one of his books, *Love Must Be Tough,* tough love means that you do what is right, not what is easy. If you really love that child, then make the decision that's best long-term for him or her, even though it may not be easy for either of you. "Correct your son, and he will give you comfort; he will also delight your soul" (Prov. 29:17). Allowing a child to be slothful, disobedient, and disrespectful is not going to help him or her in the long run. Take upon yourself the role that God has often taken with His own people. He would exile them for a period of time to help them understand their responsibilities.

I once counseled a woman whose daughter was a nurse. She lived at home but refused to help in any way and spent her money frivolously. In an effort to help discipline her daughter, the mother asked her to pay for room and board. She refused, saying, "You don't need the money. I'm not going to help you. This is as much my house as it is yours."

The mother asked her daughter to leave. When the daughter refused, the mother had some friends from church help her pack up the daughter's things and move her out.

For almost a year, the daughter was alienated from her mother, although the mother wrote regularly and told her how much she loved the daughter and that she was welcome to come back anytime she was willing to conform to the rules of her mother's home.

The daughter got married and ended up in great marital difficulty, because she adopted the same attitude toward her husband. She refused to share the money she earned or help maintain the house. She wanted to live the life of a single while she was married.

When her husband left and filed for divorce, she "woke up" and went to her mother for help. Her mother began to counsel her, and she was finally wise enough to listen. As a result, she is now a happily-married mother of three. Let me assure you that she is raising her children in a disciplined fashion, so that they will not repeat her mistakes. Love must be tough, and God says that those whom He loves, He disciplines.

Question 14:

At what age should children begin paying for their own clothes and contributing toward the family food bill, rent, and other living expenses?

I believe you have to make those decisions depending on the personality of each child. What works with one child won't work with another. I personally didn't charge my children to live at home while they were in high school or college. But if they were not going to school, I felt it was their responsibility to provide some of their own living expenses because they were adults. I didn't need the money, but I wanted them to feel that they were contributing to their own needs. I believe it gave them a greater sense of self-worth and responsibility. At some point, the same principles have to be carried over into their own families.

Question 15:

We have been managing our finances poorly and setting bad examples for our children. We want to change. We are not sure how quickly we can reverse our course and be successful with it. How fast can we go, and what is the first step?

Under no circumstances should you try to change everything as quickly as possible. You will only frustrate your children and yourselves.

I teach a seminar on the biblical principles of operating a business in which I emphasize to participants that they should not go overboard and change everything at once. They will only frustrate those around them. The same thing can happen at home.

To make financial changes at home, the parents must make some changes themselves. As a first step, a couple should thoroughly understand God's principles for managing money. It should take a maximum of twelve weeks, one half-hour per week, to learn these principles. Second, develop a realistic budget. This will probably take another three to four months. Third, bring your children into the process and help them understand the family budget. Finally, help your children establish budgets for their own funds.

I have a good friend who is fond of saying: "If it doesn't work in your life, don't export it." It's a good principle for parents to remember in applying financial goals to their children. Make it work in your life first and then help them, but don't try to change everything overnight.

Question 16:

Should we cosign for our son to buy an automobile, as he has requested, or should we give him a car instead? We are quite capable of buying our children cars.

This is not a simple, black-and-white answer, not even based on the principles of cosigning from God's Word. Proverbs 17:8a says,

"A man lacking in sense pledges." As a general principle, we are discouraged from cosigning loans.

However, parents are responsible for the debts of a minor anyway, regardless of whether they cosign or not. Regarding an adult child, it's not a good idea to cosign for a loan. A bank or any other lender requires a cosigner because it believes the borrower will not be able to repay the loan on his or her own. By cosigning, you're allowing a person to do something he or she probably can't afford to do; therefore, God probably doesn't want it to be done. I would encourage you, for these reasons, not to cosign for your children.

Should you give your child a car? That depends on the needs of the child, the utility of the car, and your conviction of what God wants you to do. In our highly mobile society, an automobile is as necessary as a horse was a hundred years ago. It's a sizeable expense, however, and you can easily go overboard by providing more car than the child needs. Some young people handle a car well, but for others it's a distraction from work or studies. As parents, you're going to have to make the decision based on these variables. There are no hard and fast rules.

Question 17:

What should we do when our parents, who are wealthy, constantly give us and our children money? We don't want it or need it. In fact, we think it's a hindrance to our being good managers of our own resources.

It won't be easy, but the best thing to do is to be honest with them. Let them know you're trying to be good money managers yourselves and would like to find out if you can make it on your own. Ask them either not to give for a while or to put the money into a trust.

I'm sure you understand that they're probably not trying to usurp your authority in your home, so be sensitive to their needs, too. This may be their way of showing love. Let them know you're aware of that. But you have a right, and a responsibility before the Lord, to be good managers yourselves.

I would also encourage you to ask them not to give directly to your children without going through you. Many times when you're trying to teach your children the right value system, a large amount of money coming from grandparents can undermine your efforts. One alternative may be to put all the money in a trust account for your children. At least that way you can delay the funds until they're old enough to manage them.

Question 18:

We are fairly well off, middle-class Americans, who have three children. They're pretty good kids, but they have adjusted to our affluent way of life. Our oldest son is rebellious and believes I should buy him a new automobile for school. He also believes I should send him to the most expensive college in the country because, he says, "You can afford it." I wasn't raised that way. I find it difficult to spend money like this when I don't think it's for the children's good. How should I respond to my son?

Too often parents yield to the weaknesses of an undisciplined or rebellious child to obtain short-term peace and to buy friendship. As Christian parents, we must accept our responsibility to stand firm in the short run to train children for the long run. We need to rely on what God's Word says, "The rod and reproof give wisdom, but a child who gets his own way brings shame to his mother" (Proverbs 29:15).

We have to establish fair but firm financial discipline early and be consistent about it. Children who get everything they ask for often become foolish, impulsive adults. These attitudes are correctable, even in older children, but it isn't easy. Often a rebellious child is testing his or her boundaries. If the boundaries are movable, the child will keep on pushing to see how far he or she can go. If the boundaries are clearly defined and fair, the child will adjust.

Contrary to what the world says, discipline does not retard a child's potential. It expands it. Remember what God says: "Whoever loves discipline loves knowledge, but he who hates reproof is stupid" (Prov. 12:1).

Set your standards and be prepared for the onslaught. It may be years before he will understand what you've done for him.

This was the case with one of my sons, who was very strong-willed. When he was a young man, it was a constant challenge to keep him in line. He joined the Marines when he was seventeen, and later I had the opportunity to visit him at his training base in California.

After we had spent a couple of hours together, he said to me, "Dad, I never thanked you for the times that you disciplined me. I didn't understand it, and I didn't appreciate it then, but I can't tell you now how much it means to me. I see many guys here who never learned self-discipline. They cry, they're depressed, and one even committed suicide."

As parents, we must always remember that God put us here to be our children's authority. We will be the ones held responsible. If you believe your actions are fair and reasonable, then stick to your guns.

Question 19:

If we are able to buy a home outright for our married children, should we do so?

This can be a great blessing, as long as you're not trying to control their lives. If it's a daughter, you need to be sure you don't usurp her husband's authority. If attitudes pose no barrier, then move ahead.

There is nothing unscriptural about buying your children homes, but you have to weigh the personalities, abilities, and attitudes of your children to ensure that you don't spoil them. However, rarely, if ever, have I seen a child spoiled as a result of having a debt-free home. But there sure have been a lot of young families wrecked because they couldn't afford the homes they bought.

Question 20:

My grown children are not handling their money properly, and my grandchildren are going without clothing, food, and other necessities. I want to help, but I don't want to interfere. Can you give some guidance?

I believe your caution shows good judgment. If God is trying to teach your children discipline and you step in, they may have to go through it all again. If you're going to help, make it contingent on your children getting professional assistance in handling their finances.

Let me add a comment here. If your children are truly needy, certainly you can help. Our own children are no less deserving of help than anybody else who is needy. However, if the income is adequate, and it's being mismanaged, you may have to be willing to let them suffer a little until they have the motivation to change.

Question 21:

I own a manufacturing company, and the desire of my heart is to bring my four children into the business. I am concerned, however, that I might not be objective and treat them fairly. Is it biblical for a son or daughter to work in a family business? How should I handle this?

Certainly it is biblical for family to be involved in a business. David passed the leadership of Israel to his son Solomon. But the children must be willing to start in positions they can handle, given their inexperience, and they shouldn't automatically expect to take over the operation. God determines talents. It's quite possible that a younger child would make a better administrator than one of your older children. Help them understand that talents are determined by

God and not you. I would also recommend that your children work outside of your business before bringing them in, so they will gain work experience from people who will treat them objectively. After you hire them, be sure you don't try to shelter any incompetence. Try hard to evaluate their performance as you would any other employee's. You can love them and still promote someone else over them if necessary. And there may come a time when they will voice disagreements about company policies. Children should have room to voice their opinions and have those opinions respected. Ultimately, if you are unable to handle them working in the business, be honest about it. The timing may be wrong for you or them.

CHAPTER 5

Lending

Even those people who think they aren't lenders often are. If you own or manage any kind of business, you're probably borrowing and lending money. A doctor who bills a patient for treatment becomes a lender. A Christian school that allows periodic payment of tuition is a lender. A parent who helps a son or daughter with a down payment on a home becomes a lender.

This section offers answers on how and when a Christian should lend money; how interest should be charged; and if collection agencies should be used for delinquent accounts. We'll also consider the question of lawsuits to collect legitimate debts.

Christians should realize from this chapter that we are unique in the way we handle our finances, even in the way God directs us to lend to others. "And if you lend to those from whom you expect to receive, what credit is that to you? Even sinners lend to sinners, in order to receive back the same amount" (Luke 6:34).

Question 1:

I work in the lending business. Should a Christian lend money to other people and charge them interest?

Christians should be concerned about two areas when it comes to lending money. First is lending to non-Christians and charging them a fair rate of interest. Second is lending to Christians and charging them any interest at all.

In Deuteronomy 23:19, we are instructed not to lend to our brothers at interest. I believe for a Christian to lend to another Christian and charge interest violates a basic principle of God's Word. We witness to others by our willingness to lend money to our brothers without profit.

No such admonition against charging interest to non-Christians exists. We're directed only to avoid excessive amounts of interest and to be fair.

If you're an employee of a company such as a savings and loan or a bank, the money you're lending is not actually your own. You're merely a representative or agent for the company. In this case, the authority to make the decisions about charging interest to anyone is not yours. You come under the authority of those for whom you work and are to follow their directions (1 Peter 2:18).

I don't personally believe a Christian is compromising who works for a company that lends money to others, including Christians, at interest, provided it's being done honestly and fairly.

However, if you believe that it's a compromise to work for a company that lends money to Christians and charges interest, I suggest you change professions.

Question 2:

I understand that we're not to charge Christians interest. Does this extend to business or investment loans? Should I really be willing to lend money to somebody else to risk in an investment without my getting any return on the money? Is this good stewardship?

This question is not easy to answer because there is little Scripture that deals with it. The implication throughout the Bible is that a loan can be made to anyone, but interest should not be charged to brothers. Whether this applies to business loans is not clear.

Obviously, no one is required to make an investment or start a business. I suggest that you pray about it and let God lead you. But in general, the principle of lending without interest to another Christian probably is applicable to any situation.

On the other hand, there may be an alternative to charging interest. You might take a percentage of the business in return for a no-interest loan. As the business prospers, your money grows with it. What would have normally been interest would become partial ownership.

Question 3:

I'm a Christian physician. I do a great deal of work for Christians in our area, and I find consistently that many of my non-pay-

ing patients are Christians. I'm concerned about what I can do to collect my money, and whether I should charge interest. I desire to do what God wants me to do, but I also want to be a good steward of the resources that God has given me. Can you help?

What you have described is unfortunately all too common. Many Christian physicians and other professionals complain that their Christian patients don't seem to feel the same compulsion to pay a Christian as they would a non-Christian. I suspect this is because they know that the non-Christian will sue and the Christian won't.

You do have the right to collect your money. If you have patients who don't pay their bills, and you believe they have the capacity to pay, confront them as prescribed in Matthew 18:15. For those who say they can't pay, send them to a Christian financial counselor in your area. Have him do a budget review for them and determine exactly how much they can pay. Every family can pay something.

As far as using a collection agency is concerned, you need to ensure that it represents the same values and principles you stand for. There is nothing unscriptural about using a collection agency unless it engages in practices you personally disagree with or that are contrary to God's Word.

If, after doing everything that you can to collect your fees, you have patients that still will not pay you, I suggest that you eliminate them from your patient schedule. I also recommend to the majority of professionals I know that they go on a cash only basis, except with patients who have demonstrated responsibility. The initial response is, "I can't possibly do that. I would lose too many of my patients." Actually, the majority of the patients they would lose are the ones who weren't going to pay in the first place.

Question 4:

Our church has a benevolence fund, but rather than giving to those in need, we lend the money, and we expect that it will be repaid. Is this unscriptural?

First let me say that Scripture does not prohibit lending to another person, even to someone in need. However, scriptural guidelines are given to us in Luke 6:34-35: "If you lend to those from whom you expect to receive, what credit is that to you? Even sinners lend to sinners in order to receive back the same amount. . . . Lend, expecting nothing in return; . . .and you will be sons of the Most High. . . ." In other words, lending in this instance is really giving because you can afford to lose the money, and you don't expect to get it back.

I believe benevolence funds should operate under two guidelines. First, the funds should help those people who are truly in need and who will, in all probability, never be able to repay. This would include: widows, orphans, and those with injuries or serious illness who can't work or generate funds to repay.

Second, the fund should be lent to those who have temporary needs or recurring needs caused by their own mismanagement. By lending to them, you're helping them establish discipline because you're asking them to repay what they owe. The loans should be without interest but should have a regular payment schedule monitored by someone on the committee.

People to whom you either lend or provide help should be made accountable to somebody who will monitor their budget at least monthly. Those who don't repay their loans should be excluded from further assistance but don't sue them or use other secular methods to collect the money.

Question 5:

I have a close relative who has borrowed money from me and not repaid it. I have loaned him money at least three times, and each time he has made a specific promise to pay me back. I would like to know what I should do.

You must seek the balance between being a good steward and being a good witness. If your relative is a Christian confront him face-to-face as you would any other Christian (see Matt. 18:15).

The best approach is honesty tempered with compassion. It's common for someone in your situation to remain silent and allow this offense to grow into bitterness. Those who owe money but can't pay are invariably embarrassed and often avoid the person they owe. Obviously that's the wrong response, but it happens. So it becomes your responsibility as the lender to approach him. If you find that he can't pay, the best course of action is to forgive all or part of the debt. If you find that he can pay but won't, confront the issue for what it is: sin.

If this is a non-Christian relative and you're concerned about your witness, consider forgiving the debt. Tell him that it's all God's money, and you're not concerned about the loss, but you are concerned about his salvation. I encourage you not to lend him more money. If he has legitimate needs, give but don't lend.

Avoid asking for monthly payments when you know he doesn't have the money. It will just add guilt and alienate him further. Above all, pray for the relative regularly, asking God to provide an opportunity to be a witness in the midst of these problems. Remember that your behavior may be the only example of Christianity this person will ever see. As the Apostle Paul wrote in Ephesians 4:32, "And be kind to one another, tender-hearted, forgiving each other, just as God in Christ also has forgiven you."

Question 6:

I understand the biblical admonition not to sue another believer, but do you believe it is all right for a Christian to sue a non-Christian for payment of a debt?

It would be simple to take the position that, since Paul warned against suing believers in 1 Corinthians 6, it must be permissible to sue non-believers. But I believe that assumption is too broad. Paul stated that suing a brother would bring shame to the church body, but he didn't imply that suing a non-believer would be acceptable.

In Luke 6:30-31, the Lord delivered a much broader principle. He said retribution is God's prerogative, not ours. God expects a high standard from us as believers, especially in our behavior toward those who are outside the faith.

We are admonished in 2 Corinthians 6:3 to give no cause for offense in anything so that the ministry might not be discredited. That doesn't mean you can never collect a debt for fear of being a bad witness. The general principle, however, is that a Christian should not sue an individual over a personal debt when it is within his or her power to forgive the debt (Matt. 5:38-42).

Question 7:

If I pass up lawsuits and forgive debts, what biblical guarantees do I have that I will not suffer from the results of my Christian approach in these matters?

Obviously, there are no such guarantees in God's Word. As Christians, we're to obey God's principles, not because we think that we can prosper from them, but because we're committed to God's way. We must be willing to respond as Shadrach, Meshach, and Abed-nego did.

When Nebuchadnezzar threatened to throw them into the furnace, they said, "If it be so, our God whom we serve is able to deliver us from the furnace of blazing fire; and He will deliver us out of your hand, O king. But even if He does not, let it be known to you, O king, that we are not going to serve your gods or worship the golden image that you have set up" (Dan. 3:17-18). We follow God's principles because we know this pleases Him. "The conclusion, when all has been heard, is: fear God and keep His commandments, because this applies to every person" (Eccl. 12:13).

Question 8:

Are there scriptural principles dealing with suing a corporation to collect a debt?

No, the Bible doesn't specifically address what to do with corporations. Therefore, you must decide what to do from another perspective.

When you're dealing with an insurance company, a bank, or any other corporation, it is an "entity." As an entity, it exists only under the law. Its officers and employees relinquish their individual rights and operate collectively under the law.

The only recourse in a dispute with many corporations is a legal one, as in the case of an insurance company. If a corporation disagrees with a settlement and refuses to pay, your only means of collecting is a lawsuit.

But before you decide to sue a corporation or any other entity, be sure of your motive. We are told in Hebrews 13:5, "Let your way of life be free from the love of money, being content with what you have." It's easy to look at any corporation with an air of detachment when it comes to suing. God always judges our attitudes, and just because something is allowable doesn't mean it's always the right thing to do.

Question 9:

If I'm sued by an individual, do I have the right to defend myself in court? Do I have the right to bring a countersuit against that individual if I believe it is necessary?

First Corinthians 6 admonishes us not to take our brothers to court. However, if someone brings a suit against you, I believe that biblically you have every right to defend yourself. Paul did so several times against the Jews and Romans, as recorded in the book of Acts.

Because another Christian sues you in violation of scriptural principles doesn't give you the right to countersue. You must be willing to put that issue in God's hands. If the lawsuit is initiated by a non-Christian, your response must be governed by what you believe to be the best witness.

Question 10:

I have tried the Matthew-18 approach of dealing with a Chris-

tian brother, but he has not responded. Are there any remedies available other than simply writing off the debt? I'm willing to do that, but I believe this individual needs to be held accountable because he hasn't paid several others. It seems to be a way of life with him.

The first step is to follow the admonition in Matthew 18 and take him before the church. If the church is not willing to step in, a group called the Christian Conciliation Council arbitrates disputes between Christians. If the other person is honest, he will be willing to put the issue in the hands of other believers. However, if he refuses, your best alternative is to write off the debt, forget about it, and do no further business with the individual.

Question 11:

I have gone bankrupt, but over the last few years I have paid back all the money I owed. Now I would like to reestablish my credit to let everybody know that I am a good credit risk. How can I do that?

It takes a long time to build a good reputation and only one problem to destroy it. Furthermore, there is no quick fix for a bad credit history. However, there are a few things you can do.

Contact each of your previous creditors and ask each of them to give you a letter, stating that you have paid your debts in full. Then ask them to contact the Credit Bureau of Chicago and give you a good credit rating. Once you have done that, it's a matter of proving you can handle credit in the future.

Obviously, God is faithful to forgive us for the violation of His principles. But that does not automatically eliminate all the consequences of our mistakes.

Although a bankruptcy action can be cleared after seven years, the legal record exists forever and is available to any inquiring creditor. The best way to clear your name is by establishing a current good credit rating.

CHAPTER 6

Borrowing and Debt

In the previous chapter we looked at lending, and now we'll consider the other side of the coin, borrowing. This topic always stimulates much discussion, because most people follow one of two extremes: abstinence or indulgence. One group thinks that borrowing is a sin and Christians should avoid it, while the other group believes that one of God's miracles is a low-interest loan. Both views are cloaked in religious folklore (something that sounds spiritual but is not scriptural).

Borrowing is an ancient concept, one discussed thoroughly in the Bible, as are many financial principles. The difficulty is that we live in an economy awash in debt, and the Bible promotes a debt-free mentality. Unfortunately, even our churches have a debt-first mentality.

Borrowing is not prohibited by Scripture, but basic rules are given for the use of it. As the questions in this chapter will reveal, most Christians have violated one or more of these rules, not out of disobedience, but out of ignorance. "The wicked borrows and does not pay back, but the righteous is gracious and gives" (Ps. 37:21).

Question 1:

I teach a class on finances in my local church, and one of my class members brought a question to me that I'm unable to answer. Can you tell me where in the Bible it says, "Neither a borrower nor a lender be"? The most important part of my question is, should Christians borrow?

The quote comes from Benjamin Franklin's *Poor Richard's Almanac*. It's not from God's Word; it's religious folklore. To answer your second question, Scripture very clearly says that neither borrowing nor lending is prohibited, but there are firm guidelines.

First, let's discuss borrowing. It's discouraged, and in fact, every biblical reference to it is a negative one. Consider Proverbs 22:7: "The rich rules over the poor, and the borrower becomes the the lender's slave."

The scriptural guideline for borrowing is very clear. When you borrow money, it's a promise to repay. Literally, borrowing is making a vow. God requires that we keep our vows. Psalm 37:21 says, "The wicked borrows and does not pay back." Therefore, if we don't want to be counted among the evil, we are to repay everything that we owe.

In biblical times, when a man borrowed money and couldn't repay, he was thrown into prison, and his family was sold into slavery. When somebody gave his word and then didn't keep it, that person greatly dishonored himself. It was worse than stealing, because a trust was violated.

Just because we don't throw people into prison today doesn't make the trust relationship any different. Scripture shows us that we're to be cautious about borrowing, and it should never be normal. Yet, when you look at our society, you find that borrowing is rampant. We think it's normal to borrow for periods of thirty to forty years. We have created an economy that borrows to exist. That is not God's way. God says in the book of Deuteronomy that borrowing is a consequence of ignoring His statutes and commandments (28:43-45).

Question 2:

We're a young married couple, and we periodically get credit cards mailed to us. I would like to have some, but my husband thinks that they're evil and that a Christian should never use them. I find it difficult even to cash a check without a credit card and almost impossible to rent a car. Is it wrong to have credit cards?

Credit cards are not evil, and they're not the problem. The problem is the misuse of credit cards. Most children see their parents use credit cards to buy clothes, gas, food, and even toys. But very few parents bring their children in when they write the checks and say, "Kids, remember when we charged all that stuff? Now we have to pay for it."

I find that credit cards, although not essential, can be a great convenience. But let me give you some simple guidelines that will help you avoid difficulty.

As husband and wife, together, you should make some very simple vows: 1) Never use your credit cards to buy anything that is not in your budget for the month. So first, you should have a budget. (See Chapter 3 for budget guidelines.) 2) Pay your credit cards off every month with no exception. 3) The first month you're unable to pay the credit cards, destroy them. If you take these vows, you'll never have a problem with credit cards.

Question 3:

How can we as Christians teach our children principles of borrowing and lending? At what age should we begin that education process? Do you publish any material covering the subject?

Yes, I do have material covering the subject. The workbook is called *God's Guide Through the Money Jungle* and is suitable for children ages nine through fourteen.

Also, you can begin teaching your teenagers the principles of borrowing and lending by giving them a real-life opportunity to handle credit. Allow them to have credit cards under very strict supervision (for more on this, see chapter 4). We need to teach our children how to handle credit, not how to avoid it, since they will be exposed to all kinds of easy credit once they leave home. It's far better to teach them the proper use of credit before they leave our control.

You also should teach your children the principles of interest and how various interest forms work. Teach them the difference between simple, compound, and add-on interest. One of the best ways to do this is to visit your local library and check out a book on consumer economics. Use this as a part of your devotional series for a while. There will be no better investment that you can make in your children than spending time teaching them how to handle money properly.

Credit is the major problem for young couples. It's the motivating factor behind perhaps eighty percent of all divorces. You can help your children avoid a lot of grief by teaching them properly while they are at home. "By wisdom a house is built, and by understanding it is established; and by knowledge the rooms are filled with all precious and pleasant riches" (Prov. 24:3-4).

Question 4:

Could you define debt? If I owe two hundred dollars a month on a car, and I can afford the payment, am I legitimately in debt? Or does debt refer just to an amount I owe that I can't afford to repay?

To define debt is not simple, but basically it's an obligation to pay that cannot be met. When you borrow money, we traditionally say, "You're in debt." But if you're able to make each payment, you aren't in debt. When you can't pay what you've promised, then you're in debt.

Probably forty percent of all American families are in debt in a typical year. They're unable to make the monthly payments on the money they borrowed. Many actually borrow more money to make payments on the money they've already borrowed.

The number-one cause of indebtedness for young couples is housing. A couple buys a house too expensive for their budget, and the house strips them of cash they will need for other things. Because they don't have cash to keep their car repaired, they end up buying a new car. That strips them of even more cash, and then they go into debt for necessities such as food, clothing, and medical expenses.

Indebtedness is difficult for anybody to handle. It will destroy a relationship between husband and wife and between a Christian and God. You can't have a good relationship with your spouse when all you ever talk about are problems. When you sit down to read God's Word and nothing comes to mind except problems, you don't read very much. When you sit down to pray and all you can think about are problems, you stop praying. In our society so many people are in debt that we accept it as normal. It certainly is not biblical.

Question 5:

*We have overspent for the last three or four years, and it has
finally caught up with us. We've gone through bill consolidation
loans, loans from parents, and equity loans. Now we find ourselves
unable to pay our bills again. We have overdue credit card bills,
but we're using credit cards just to live month by month. How can
we get out of this mess?*

Let me share with you one of the simplest economic principles
ever written: "If you don't borrow money, you can't get into debt."
The second simplest economic principle is, "If you don't borrow
any more money, you can't get further into debt."

So the first thing you have to say is, "I'm not going to go any
further into debt." It's really a matter of deciding, "Do I trust God,
or do I just say that I trust God?" Any couple in debt must begin
reversing the process that got them there. If you find you're overspending month by month on your credit cards, destroy them, and
mail them back in little pieces.

Next, make out a budget that will control your spending as
much as possible, but be realistic about it. Don't promise to pay
more than you're able to. Write each of your creditors a letter,
show them your budget, and how much money you have available.
Give them a list of all the other creditors and divide your money
proportionately.

If you're only able to pay half of what you originally promised,
tell them the truth. I've negotiated with many creditors for counselees, and I can tell you that lenders don't want somebody to go
bankrupt. All they want is their money. I have never found a lender
(other than some small loan companies) who would not work
things out with a family as long as the family was honest and was
running toward its creditors.

Running toward those we owe rather than away from them is
one of the principles taught in Scripture. Matthew 5:25 says,
"Make friends quickly with your opponent at law while you are
with him on the way; in order that your opponent may not deliver
you to the judge, and the judge to the officer, and you be thrown

into prison." That means making this commitment: "I'm not to go any further into debt. I'll be honest with my creditors. I'll sacrifice what I have to, and I'll pay back what I've promised."

Then it becomes God's responsibility to help. The average family should be able to be debt-free in about two years (other than those with business or investment losses).

Once you've made a commitment to pay your creditors what you can each month, make another commitment. If any additional money comes in, use at least half of it to pay on your debts. Work hardest to pay off your smallest debt first. Then take all the money you were paying on that bill and put it toward the next largest one. In this way you'll see your debts begin to disappear. Anyone who ever got into debt knows getting there is a lot of fun. It's not nearly as much fun getting out.

Question 6:

We're a family of four, making less than $15,000 a year. We have an extremely hard time staying out of debt. No matter how hard we try, every time we get one bill paid off, something else breaks down, and we're right back in debt again. Can you help us?

There's really only one way out. Discipline yourselves not to go into debt. One of the greatest dangers for a low-income family is to use consumer credit, especially credit cards. Unless you're very disciplined, you probably should not use credit cards at all.

Furthermore, you need to make out a budget that balances income and outgo, even if you must sacrifice a car, house, or private school. Be sure to allow some money for every category of expense (refer to the chapter 2 on budgeting). Then if you have an added expense (and you probably will), you must believe that God has an answer that does not require you to borrow money.

A part of God's solution is other Christians. When you have a legitimate need, you must let others in your church know.

Isn't it strange that in Christianity we have great freedom to share physical problems, but practically no freedom to share financial problems? Yet God's Word says ten times as much about finances as it does about physical needs. "At this present time your abundance being a supply for their want, that their abundance also may become a supply for your want, that there may be equality" (2 Cor. 8:14).

Question 7:

My family income exceeds $75,000 a year, ten times what I earned when I started my career ten years ago. Yet it seems every month we go further into debt. Is this normal with high-income families?

Let me mention what happened during some of my early counseling. One day I met with a couple who were having financial problems. I asked them, "Tell me what you think the problem is."

They responded, "We don't make enough money. Our total income is only about $15,000 a year, and that's not enough to live on in this area."

I gave them a budget form and had them write down everything they were spending. Sure enough, $15,000 was not enough for them to live on. As they left, I gave them some material to read before the next session.

The next couple came in. I asked them the same question: "What do you think your problem is?"

The husband said, "We only make about $25,000 a year, and that's not enough money to live on in this area."

So I had them fill out the budget form, and sure enough, $25,000 was not enough money.

The next couple came in, and I asked them the same question.

Their problem was, the husband said, "We're only making $75,000 a year, and that is not enough money to buy what we need."

They filled out the same budget form, and sure enough, they didn't make enough money.

If I could have given that first couple, making $15,000 a year, a $75,000 income, they would have left thinking themselves the wealthiest couple in town. I also believe they would have been back in about two years, having overspent their new income level.

The truth is, the amount of money you make is not relevant; it's the amount of money you spend. High-income families end up in debt as well as low-income families.

I remember a professional athlete I was counseling, who was making more than $250,000 a year. Yet every year he went into debt.

I asked, "Why can't you live on a quarter of a million dollars?"

He said, "It's impossible. I've tried everything I can. We just can't make it."

He was about two years out of college, so I asked him, "How much did you make in your last year of college?"

He said, "Oh, about $2,500."

I asked, "How did you live on it?"

He replied, "Well, it was all that I had."

Right! You see, he got by because he had no more money to spend. Nobody would lend him money, because he was in such a low-income bracket. It boils down to self-discipline, not how much you make.

Question 8:

Do you think that Christians should be totally debt free, including their homes? What if I have enough money to pay off my home, but the mortgage carries a low, six percent interest rate? I can make nearly twice that by keeping my mortgage and investing my money elsewhere. Is it logical to pay off my home?

God wants His people to be debt free. Debt is not normal, according to God's Word, and long-term debt is totally abnormal. I see no indication in Scripture that any debt ever extended beyond seven years. It's only in our era that we have made long-term debt normal.

Take the matter of housing. Suppose that you owned a $100,000 home, and the law changed so that you were unable to sell your house to anybody through a mortgage. In other words, they had to pay cash for it. What do you think your $100,000 home would be worth? $75,000? $50,000? Probably closer to $25,000 or $30,000. The cost of that house is inflated through borrowing.

I believe everyone should own his home debt free. If I had to choose to either invest my money and earn ten percent, or to pay off a six percent mortgage, I would pay off the mortgage. Who knows what might happen in the economy that could destroy your investments? And yet the mortgage payments would keep right on going. Remember, what you own belongs to you, and nobody can take it from you.

I've heard accountants say it's illogical to pay off your home because you lose the interest from tax write-offs. But when you look at it logically, that doesn't make much sense. Let's assume you're in a thirty percent tax bracket right now. If you pay $1,000 in interest, you'll get back approximately $300 in refunded tax. What happened to the other $700? As best I know, somebody kept it. If you think that's a good deal, I'll make you a better one. If you'll send me $1,000, I'll mail you back $900, in which case you get back three times your tax write-off.

Anytime you pay interest you lose. One of the best ways to pay off a home is to begin accelerating the mortgage. If, for instance, you have a $70,000 mortgage on your home for thirty years, you're going to pay back well in excess of $200,000 for that mortgage, the difference being interest. If you could just pay an extra $100 a month on your loan, you would retire your mortgage in fifteen years, saving fifteen years of payments and more than $70,000 in interest.

It makes a lot of sense to be debt free. It can be done. Granted, the average couple can't buy a home debt free, but if they're willing to discipline themselves and pay off that mortgage, almost any couple in the United States can be debt free in ten to fifteen years.

Question 9:

I have heard the word "surety" used many times in financial discussions. What does it mean?

"Surety" is a biblical term. You'll find it used regularly in the book of Proverbs. For instance, Proverbs 17:18 says, "A man lacking in sense pledges, and becomes surety in the presence of his neighbor."

"Surety" means standing as guarantor for a debt. An example of surety in Scripture would be cosigning. Cosigning means you pledge to pay the obligations of another person. He borrowed money and you signed the note, so if he doesn't pay, you have to.

Surety is one of the most commonly violated money management principles. Almost everybody who borrows signs surety. For instance, if you finance an automobile, you sign surety. The lender knows that the automobile is rarely going to be worth what is owed on it. Yet the loan agreement requires that you, the buyer, guarantee any deficiency if the car is repossessed and resold. Thus, the buyer stands surety.

How can you avoid surety? Probably only one way. Have collateral that can be surrendered in total payment of the debt. Suppose you bought land that cost $10,000, and you put $1,000 down and borrowed $9,000. The terms of your contract stipulate, "If ever I can't pay for this land, I give you the right to take the land back and keep all the money that I paid in, but I am released from all liabilities." Then you avoid surety. It was collateralized, and you had a certain way to pay.

Proverbs says the man who lacks sense will sign surety (17:18). The obvious reason is because many times surety will come back to haunt you when you can least afford it.

Question 10:

I've heard that it's all right to borrow in times of high inflation or to borrow for appreciating assets, such as a house, since they're always worth more than what is owed. Do you agree?

The difficulty in borrowing during appreciating times is that suddenly you may enter depreciating times. The classic examples are the oil and farming industries. For decades many farms were operated debt free. Then during the inflationary period of the '70s and early '80s, farmland began to appreciate greatly. Many farmers borrowed against the appreciating land values to buy more land and better equipment. But then, when food prices fell and their crops couldn't be sold at the prices they expected, the price of the land dropped drastically. Unfortunately, the debt still existed. As a result, thousands of farmers lost everything.

When borrowing against an appreciating asset, you don't know if it's going to continue to appreciate. Many people think that if they borrow only for a home, they're all right, because it will go up in value. If you think that's true, you should have visited Houston in the mid-'80s when the oil industry collapsed and the value of housing dropped by half. Many people lost their homes because they couldn't be sold at any price. God's principles are not determined by the economy. They're determined by His wisdom.

So, should you ever borrow to buy a house? Unfortunately, because of debt-generated inflation, most families have to borrow for a house. The wise response to this situation is to make a commitment to pay off the loan as rapidly as possible. The sooner you pay off your home, the sooner it belongs to you and not to a bank.

Question 11:

I'm from a school of thought that says use other people's money; in other words, borrow to do whatever you want. It's a hard mentality to shake, even though I now understand it's contrary to God's Word. I was recently at a meeting in which fund raisers recommended that people in a congregation borrow to give to the church building program. That sounds more reasonable to me than the church itself borrowing. What do you think?

If you knowingly violate biblical principles, it's wrong, no matter how noble the purpose. I don't believe God would direct anyone to violate His Word to accomplish His work. The principle of surety says that we're not to borrow against an unknown contingency.

The idea of using other people's money has been greatly overplayed in our society, especially within the church. I believe that God has provided us Christians all the money necessary to do anything we want, if we're committed to it. Borrowing should never play a part in giving. We should always give what belongs to us, not what belongs to somebody else. I would encourage you not to borrow needlessly, even to give to your church.

Question 12:

What does the word "collateral" mean?

"Collateral" is an asset that is pledged by a borrower as security for a loan. If the loan is not repaid, the asset becomes the lender's, and the borrower forfeits all further rights to the collateral.

Question 13:

We're a young couple, and we've just opened our first checking account. The banker told us about a helpful service called "automatic overdraft protection." He said if we ever overdraw our checking account, the automatic overdraft covers the deficiency. This seems like a good idea, but I know that it must have some pitfalls. Can you help us understand it better?

Beware of automatic overdrafts. They present two distinct problems: 1) They encourage people not to balance their checking accounts because they know that they have overdraft "protection." 2) An automatic overdraft is also an automatic loan. It comes out of a credit account, and you're charged interest as well as a fee for using it.

Not long ago I counseled a young couple who had charged almost $600 on their automatic overdraft. To their dismay, they got a bill from the bank for $600 plus interest.

The wife told me, "I didn't know it was a loan. I thought it was one of the courtesies the bank extended."

You may be thinking, "Nobody is that naive." But let me assure you, many people are that naive.

In my opinion, the automatic overdraft is one of the worst services in banking and certainly one of quickest sources of debt for undisciplined couples who don't balance their checkbooks. A proverb says it well: "The naive proceed and pay the penalty" (Prov. 27:12b).

Question 14:

Larry, isn't there a difference between personal debt—that is, buying things for the family—and business loans? How could anybody operate a major business in America today without using credit?

I would disagree. I don't think it's anymore essential for a business to borrow money than it is for an individual. Granted, it's convenient, and there are circumstances where using credit can be beneficial. But I know many Christians who operate their businesses debt free.

One way to avoid debt is to bring in money from investors. In other words, sell equity in your business rather than borrow. That was the most common method of funding a business prior to World War II.

I don't see any essential difference in God's Word between personal debt and business debt. That doesn't mean you can't borrow. It simply means that when you do, you assume a liability and the associated risks. Having counseled many couples with enormous debts from failed businesses, I can tell you it creates a financial burden that can wreck your health and your family.

So be very careful about any debt, especially in a business. Establish the goal of eventually being debt-free, including your business. Don't be trapped into believing that indebtedness is normal. It's not.

Question 15:

Our laws permit individuals to declare bankruptcy rather than have to remain in debt the rest of their lives. Do you think this is a proper course of action for a Christian? How about a Chapter 13 bankruptcy, in which the individual is required eventually to repay the creditors?

Simply because something is legal doesn't make it acceptable. As far as I can determine from God's Word, bankruptcy is not an option for a Christian. If someone is forced into involuntary bankruptcy by creditors, nothing can be done about it. But even then, a Christian is obligated to pay the debt in full (Ps. 37:21).

Chapter 13 of the bankruptcy law is actually called a "personal reorganization," very similar to a Chapter 11 bankruptcy for a corporation. Under Chapter 13, the individual is not necessarily required to pay all the debt; the court may elect to dissolve any or all of it. It would not be unusual for a judge to dissolve fifty percent of the debt, leaving the creditors with less than full value.

I can find no reason why Christians couldn't take advantage of Chapter 13, provided they committed to continue paying until all debts are resolved.

A stigma is attached to all bankruptcy, including Chapter 13. Once you have gone bankrupt, there is virtually no way to remove that mark from your record. Under the pressures of heavy debt, bankruptcy seems like the only way out. But, in reality, many people go bankrupt when they could have worked out an alternative.

Most creditors don't want someone to go bankrupt, because then everybody loses. If you approach your creditors with total honesty and a willingness to sacrifice to pay as much as possible, they will work with you. But often someone starts out with good intentions and then doesn't pay regularly; the creditors get tired of empty promises. Remember, God's Word says, "A good name is to be more desired than great riches" (Prov. 22:1a).

Question 16:

I'm a Christian who has filed for bankruptcy. I've lost every-

*thing I own: my business, material possessions, even my family.
There's no way I can ever climb out of the hole I'm in. I owed
hundreds of thousands of dollars that were erased through the
bankruptcy. I can see no way that I will ever be able to pay it
back. This problem has ruined relationships with a lot of friends
and family who lost their money in my business. Do you think
there's hope for me? Can I be an effective witness for the Lord
while I still owe all this money? What if I never can pay it all
back?*

God's Word is so simple. First John 1:9 says, "If we will confess our sins [which means agree with God], He is faithful and
righteous to forgive us our sins and to cleanse us from all unrigh-
teousness."

God can use anyone; it doesn't matter whether that person is in
or out of debt, provided that individual's heart is right. I also believe no situation is hopeless. Although you may not see the solution, I've watched God work many times when there seemed to be
no visible answer.

I recall a businessman who had been cheating on his income
taxes for years. After hearing God's Word, he was convicted about
his dishonesty. He turned himself in to the Internal Revenue
Service, and as best they could determine, he owed more than a
million dollars in back taxes. His business could never generate the
kind of profit necessary to pay that back. But since he could only
do what he could do, he began to pay. The IRS actually put a re-
ceiver in charge of his business to collect the money, pay his salary
and bills, and pay the rest to the government. That continued for
almost three years.

Then one day I received a letter from him which began, "Praise
the Lord!" A major oil company had struck oil on his property, in
the middle of his parking lot. The royalties from the well were
enough to pay the back taxes, and within five years he was debt
free. Who could have anticipated how that debt would be paid?
Certainly not me. I encourage you to own up to your debts, pay
back what you can, and trust God.

Question 17:

In reading through the Bible, I found Romans 13:8 which says, "Owe nothing to anyone except to love one another; for he who loves his neighbor has fulfilled the law." Does this mean that God never wants a Christian to borrow money?

My interpretation of Romans 13:8 is that the Apostle Paul was not referring directly to money. He was saying, don't let people do something for you unless you're willing to do even more for them. If Paul had been specifically telling Christians to never borrow money, I believe he would have made it absolutely clear, because then he would have been countermanding many other Scriptures that deal with borrowing money. Borrowing or lending are not scripturally prohibited. We need to be careful not to build a doctrine out of a single verse but to take Scripture as a whole.

Question 18:

Do you believe that a Christian may borrow money from a non-Christian, or is that prohibited scripturally?

God's Word simply says that whatever is borrowed must be repaid. It doesn't specify whether a believer should borrow from another believer or from a non-believer. It doesn't make any difference, as far as repayment is concerned. A caution appears in Proverbs 22:7 in which we are told that a lender becomes an authority over a borrower. That might be particularly important where a church or another ministry is concerned.

Question 19:

Is a lease actually the same thing as a loan, particularly where a lease for an automobile is concerned?

A lease is basically no different from a loan. When you sign a lease, it's a contingent liability and an obligation to pay. For instance, if you lease a car and for some reason during the term of the lease you can't make the payments and give the automobile back, you will still owe the difference between the sale value and the remaining lease. It's called a deficiency agreement. Once a lease contract is signed, you have an obligation to pay that is just as binding as a loan. You don't avoid surety by leasing.

In general, I believe the economics of a lease are usually bad and actually more costly than a loan. Many young couples today are leasing automobiles primarily because they can't afford the down payment on a new car. Unfortunately, they probably can't afford a new car under any terms. Leasing a car they can't afford to buy doesn't avoid the problem.

Question 20:

If God doesn't want Christians to go into debt, does that make a home mortgage wrong?

God's Word doesn't prohibit borrowing. It's almost a certainty that most couples will have to borrow for their first home. With the exception of a few states that don't allow deficiency agreements on home mortgages, borrowers will have to sign surety. This means that if the house were repossessed and sold at a loss, the borrower would still have to make up the deficiency.

However, I also know that in our current situation, for a young couple to buy a house, they will have to have a mortgage. To take out a mortgage, they must sign surety. It's important to realize that surety is not a law but a principle. You have a right to do it, but a risk is involved. You can lose everything because of surety, including other assets.

Therefore, try to avoid the consequences of surety by making certain the asset is worth more than what you owe. If you borrow to buy a home, make a commitment to pay it off as rapidly as possible, or at least to reduce the mortgage to the point where the house is worth more than you owe.

Question 21:

I understand we can prepay our mortgage and reduce expenses significantly. How does this work?

During the early years of your mortgage, a small portion of each monthly payment goes toward the principle, while the majority goes toward interest. But any additional money you pay each month goes entirely toward the principle. Therefore, the next month you're paying off slightly less interest and slightly more principle on the unpaid balance.

Whenever you send an extra mortgage payment, mark your check clearly, "To be applied to principle payment only." If you do this regularly, you can significantly reduce the number of years you pay on your mortgage and save a tremendous amount of interest.

Question 22:

What are the advantages and disadvantages of refinancing our home if the prevailing interest rates are lower than our mortgage rate?

Many people refinance when they can get a lower interest rate. However, you need to consider the additional costs. First, you will have to pay a loan origination fee for a new loan, and you may have a pay-off penalty on the old loan. Plus, you will incur attorney's fees, closing costs, etc.

If you plan to stay in the home for a long period of time, typically more than three years, you can recover the costs through the lower interest rate (provided the new rate is at least two percent less than the old one). But if you intend to sell the home in the near future, you may actually give up a benefit. Your old loan may be assumable, even though it's a higher rate, and the new loan may not be. So if the rates go up again and you try to sell your home, you may have a difficult time because the buyer would be forced to pay the prevailing interest rate.

Generally, if you plan to live in your home for several years and you can lower the interest rate by refinancing, it's a good idea.

Question 23:

I'm an eighty-one-year-old widow, and I live on a fixed income which just barely meets my needs. My home has been paid off for almost twenty-five years. Its value has increased greatly, and a friend in my church suggested that I borrow out of the equity, invest it, and use the capital to live on. Are there any guidelines to let me know whether this is a good idea?

Yes, one of the guidelines comes out of Proverbs. In paraphrase, Proverbs 15:22 says, "It's a wise man who seeks many counselors." Also in paraphrase, Proverbs 14:15 says, "A fool believes whatever he is told."

At eighty-one years of age, I don't think it's a good idea to borrow on your home, unless you're willing to move in the event that something happens. No matter where your funds are invested, they can be lost, given the wrong set of circumstances. The debt on your house will continue regardless. So I would encourage you, especially at your age, not to borrow on your home.

I believe borrowing equity from a home is some of the worst advice ever given. The majority of people that I know who have done so, have ended up spending or losing the money. All they have left to show for it is more debt on their home.

The first question any Christian has to ask is, "Do I consider my house just another investment?" With rare exception, a house is not an investment. It's a purchase. So don't treat it like an investment, unless you're selling an expensive house and moving to a less expensive one. Then you can treat the profit as investment capital without risking your home.

Question 24:

Is it true that any debt, including a mortgage, that exceeds six years is scripturally forbidden?

I don't know that I would use the word "forbidden"; a better word might be "discouraged." According to the book of Deuteronomy, the year of remission came every seventh year (15:1). During that year, all debts to "brothers" were to be released. Therefore, the longest debt was indeed six years.

However, the admonition to release a debt was always to the lender, not the borrower. Therefore, you don't have a right to go to a lender and say, "Listen, I've had this loan seven years. I'm not going to pay you anymore." If you try that today, you'll end up with your property repossessed. The principle is given to encourage God's people to avoid thinking that long-term debt is normal. It is not.

Question 25:

My wife and I made a commitment to get out of debt, but we owe a lot—on credit cards and to small loan companies—and all of it comes at a high interest rate. Is it logical for us to consolidate those loans into one loan at a smaller interest rate? Should we use the equity in our home as well?

It does make more sense to consolidate your debts at a lower interest rate, but not immediately. First develop a budget to control your spending. Then commit yourself to living on it for six months without borrowing any more. Otherwise, all you're doing with a consolidation loan is treating the symptom and not the problem. When you know that you can live without credit, then consider consolidation.

An equity loan may be the best interest rate you can get. It's the most logical choice because you are using the equity to substitute for higher interest loans. But be certain that the loan has a fixed interest rate and not a floating rate.

However, you need to pray about it with your wife to be sure that you both agree. With rare exception, most women don't want to borrow on the equity in their homes. To them, a home represents security and comfort, not a source of money.

Question 26:

We've been looking into various ways to buy a home and see two options. One is a fixed-rate loan, the other is a variable-rate loan. Fixed-rate loans are more difficult to obtain, and many times the fees associated with them are higher. We can get a variable-rate loan at about two percent less annually than the fixed rate, and the variable rate does have a cap so that it can never go more than three and one-half points above the initial rate. It can't be increased more than one percent per year. Which is the better way to finance?

Adjustable Rate Mortgages (ARMs) are relatively new. The key to an ARM is to remember that it's adjustable. Plan accordingly. If you can get an ARM at a lower rate than a fixed-rate loan, and you're absolutely sure that you could make the payments at the higher rate should it rise, go with the variable-rate loan. Logically, if the fixed-rate loan is two percent higher than the ARM and the ARM can only increase three and one-half percent, then the most you have at risk is the additional one and one-half percent. Since that would be phased in over three years, it's worth the risk.

Many couples, however, have taken on ARMs without rate caps. Some of these can increase virtually forever. They are ticking time bombs, and I recommend those loans be converted as rapidly as possible to either a fixed-rate or an adjustable-rate loan with a cap.

Question 27:

My wife and I want our sons to attend college, but we don't make enough money to pay for it. I could qualify for a home equity loan that would pay at least the first two years. Could you give us counsel?

Proverbs 22:7 says, "The rich rules over the poor, and the borrower becomes the lender's slave." When you borrow money, regardless of what you use it for, you potentially become a servant to the lender. If you desire to borrow money to send your children to school, that's your decision. Borrowing for college is more logical than borrowing to buy a car. But it's still a loan that can cost you your home.

So be sure you weigh the costs carefully. "For which one of you, when he wants to build a tower, does not first sit down and calculate the cost, to see if he has enough to complete it?" (Luke 14:28).

God promises that He will provide what we need. "And my God shall supply all your needs according to His riches in glory in Christ Jesus" (Phil. 4:19). As best I can tell, God has never manifested Himself to anybody through a loan.

If you're unable to pay your children's way to college, look for alternatives. Perhaps they could go to a community or a junior college for a couple of years. Then perhaps they could get into a work program with a company that will help them go to college. Scholarships and grants are also available to good students. Many of these go unclaimed because students would rather borrow and not have to work.

I've counseled many young people who finished college owing tremendous amounts of money. They ended up working the next ten years trying to get out of debt. That doesn't mean that borrowing is evil, but it does demonstrate that Christians are as caught up in the "world" as anybody else.

Remember that college loans, like any loans, restrict God's ability to direct us. What if God has an alternate plan for financing your children's college education, but you don't ever explore it because of readily available loans? Or what if your children should not go to college right now? Those are questions that only you, as parents, and your children, can answer before the Lord.

Question 28:

Do you believe that it's advisable for a church to borrow money, even for a building program?

The only source of truth we have is God's Word. Anything else is opinion. As I look into God's Word, I don't see an example of a church or related organization borrowing for any reason, including a building. That doesn't mean borrowing is a sin. It's just that borrowing is the least acceptable alternative, and God would not have His church accept the least.

Clearly the church has to live by a higher standard than even its individual members, because it stands totally as a demonstration of God's power and omnipotence. Unfortunately, faith isn't demonstrated when the church indebts itself to do God's work. Deuteronomy 15:4-6 says that if we obey and trust God, we will not have to borrow money. We will be lenders.

Many Christians will argue that it's all right to borrow because, they say, "We need to get God's work done right now. Besides, it's for an appreciating asset." It doesn't matter whether it is for an appreciating asset or a depreciating asset. A debt is a debt.

Scripture says that the borrower becomes the lender's slave, and I find it hard to believe that God would have his church indebted to the secular world, particularly to a bank. Borrowing is not a necessity. There is no lack of money within Christianity. God has given us enough to do everything we have to do; the problem is a lack of willingness to give. Giving, or the lack of it, on the part of God's people is an external sign of an internal spiritual condition.

I remember one Sunday when I was about to speak to a church that was in the middle of a building program. I met with the pastor and the board of deacons before the service. One of the questions I asked them was, "Why are you going to borrow money?"

The chairman of the deacon board responded, "What do you mean, 'Why are we going to borrow money?' We're going to borrow because we don't have the money to build."

So my next question was, "Well, if you did have it, would you still borrow?"

Obviously, if they had the money in the bank and were still going to borrow, it would not be an issue of need but a commitment to debt.

He said, "No, if we had the money, we wouldn't borrow."

Then I asked the pastor, "Pastor, if I could prove to you that you have all the money you need to build, would you make a commitment to do it debt free?"

He said, "Yes, I believe that we would."

About six hundred people attended the church that morning. During the service I took a quick financial survey.

I said, "I'd like to know how many people in the congregation own at least one ounce of gold in their family, including rings, earrings, watches, etc." Almost every hand in the church went up.

"Okay," I continued, "how many families believe they own at least ten ounces of silver, including silverware, flatware, candlesticks?"

Again, almost every hand went up. That happened to be at the time when gold and silver were at a very high premium. I turned to the pastor and said, "Pastor, as best as I can calculate, you have every dollar you need in this congregation this morning to build your church. Now I showed you they've got it; you figure out how to get it from them."

Borrowing to build a church simply avoids the necessity of God's people giving, and I believe it robs them of one of God's blessings, according to 2 Corinthians 9:6-8. Borrowing is also a manifestation of a lack of understanding of God's promises, because God has committed Himself to provide us with everything we need, and even an abundance above that for every good deed.

Question 29:

We're about to begin a building program in our church. I believe that we should not borrow from the secular world, but a group has come in to help us and suggested we issue church bonds to our own people. Since we're not borrowing from the secular world, and we're going to be indebted to each other, is there a scriptural prohibition against this?

In the context of lending the church money and charging interest, I believe church bonds are not scriptural. Deuteronomy 23:19 says not to lend to a brother at interest, and certainly this would apply to a church loan. If the people would lend without interest, then I believe the scriptural principle would not be violated.

We aren't the owners of wealth and money; we're managers of it for God (Luke 16:10-13). It would be difficult to understand how a Christian could lend money to our Master and then charge Him interest on His own money. I believe church bonds are biblical, but charging the church interest is not.

CHAPTER 7

Giving

Question 20: How should I decide which Christian organizations to give to?

Question 21: How should I respond to Christian organizations that beg by mail?

Question 22: How can I learn whether money I send is used properly?

Question 23: Should I contribute directly to a needy individual?

Question 24: Should I give to a beggar?

Question 25: What about charitable organizations that solicit in airports and malls?

Question 26: Can I earmark my tithe for specific purposes?

Question 27: Is it better to lend or to give to a friend in need?

Question 28: Are there advantages to donating appreciated assets rather than cash?

Question 29: When I contribute to an organization and receive a premium, how much of my contribution is tax deductible?

Question 30: How does a church benevolence program work?

When most Christians think about giving, it's almost always related to the tithe. But Christians face other decisions about giving, too. In this chapter, we will discuss the basic questions, and then cover other matters dealing with giving.

One exciting benefit of scriptural giving is that it allows a family to see God prove Himself faithful, as He has promised. The Bible says one doesn't grow closer to God by giving. Instead, giving is a sign of someone who is already close to God. "For I testify that according to their ability, and beyond their ability they gave of their own accord, begging us with much entreaty for the favor of participation in the support of the saints" (2 Cor. 8:3-4).

Question 1:

Do you believe it's necessary for a Christian to give in secret, as Matthew 6:3-4 says? If so, should we claim our gifts on our income tax?

Remember that in every scriptural lesson Christ deals with our motives and attitudes, as well as with our actions. The admonition to give in secret is directed at those people who have a difficult time with the sin of pride.

In Matthew 6:6 the Lord said, ". . .When you pray, go into your inner room, and when you have shut your door, pray to your Father who is in secret, and your Father who sees in secret will repay you." And yet we know of instances in which we are directed to pray together openly. These would appear to be contradictory statements. How can two or more pray together (Matt. 18:19-20), and yet each be directed to pray secretly? Obviously, Christ is dealing with attitudes.

Those people who pray so that they might be noticed by others are directed to go into their closets and pray. Those who don't have that problem can pray in public. Those who give so others might notice them should never give publicly. They should give anonymously. If giving to be recognized is not a problem in your life, then give as God leads you. Open giving can bond Christians together and can be a demonstration to other people of how God wants them to give.

Whether or not you decide to claim your contribution on your income tax return is a matter of personal conviction. If you don't want to profit from your giving, I would suggest giving your tax savings as well.

Question 2:

Do you believe that Christians should give up every material possession and monetary surplus to serve the Lord? More specifically, how do you interpret Matthew 19:21, in which Jesus said, "If you wish to be complete, go and sell your possessions and give to the poor, and you shall have treasure in heaven; and come, follow Me"?

I would direct you to 2 Corinthians 8:13 in which Paul wrote, ". . .This is not for the ease of others and for your affliction, but by way of equality." In other words, the purpose of giving is to satisfy needs, not to create new ones. I see no instance in Scripture in which someone is directed to give away everything, except when the person had a problem with his attitude toward possessions. If you have a balanced attitude toward material things, then God will give you more to give away. Proverbs 30:8-9 says, "Give me neither poverty nor riches, feed me with the food that is my portion, lest I be full and deny Thee and say 'Who is the Lord?' Or lest I be in want and steal, and profane the name of my God."

God's main concern for each of us is our attitude. Paul wrote, ". . . I have learned to be content in whatever circumstances I am. I know how to get along with humble means, and I also know how to live in prosperity . . ." (Phil. 4:11-12).

Obviously, if you have an attitude that needs to be corrected, God may well direct you to give away everything and learn to trust Him. But if you can handle material things and keep life in balance, you can use your resources to multiply the kingdom of God. Each of us must live a disciplined life, learn to budget our money, and be gracious givers, but not to the point of giving away everything.

Quite often a new believer will feel the need to give away everything and go to the mission field. That's usually when the wife, who had been the giver in the family, panics. Almost always this desire to give away everything is born out of guilt and repentance. Paul tells us, "Let each one do just as he has purposed in his heart; not grudgingly or under compulsion; for God loves a cheerful giver" (2 Cor. 9:7). One sign that God wants somebody to give everything away is that that person will have a cheerful spirit before, during, and after, and the spouse agrees. Matthew 19:21 is meant to challenge the casual follower with the fact that Christ wants only those who are totally committed to Him.

Question 3:

What should we do if we feel we can't trust our church to handle money well? I don't mean to say they're doing anything illegal or immoral; we just don't like the way money is managed. The church leaders seem to waste a great deal of it, and we don't feel comfortable giving any more.

This question can be answered on the basis of what Luke 16:10-11 says, "He who is faithful in a very little thing is faithful also in much; and he who is unrighteous in a very little thing is unrighteous also in much. If therefore you have not been faithful in the use of unrighteous Mammon, who will entrust the true riches to you?" If you truly believe you can't entrust your money to your church, you shouldn't stay there. However, I would say that first you should examine your own motives.

Why do you feel that you can't trust your church with your money? Is it because you disagree with the way the church leaders are spending it? I may disagree with the way you spend your money, and you would most probably disagree with the way I spend mine. That's not a valid reason to withhold support from your church. The only biblical reason for not financially supporting your church is that you find it deceitful, dishonest, or in some other way unbiblical. If you have evidence of that, you need to go immediately to the church's leadership, present your evidence, and give the leaders a chance to respond.

If you disagree with how the leadership spends money, you have a right to voice your opinion, but remember that it is your opinion, not necessarily the right one. Scripture requires you to support those who teach you, which means you should support your local church (Gal. 6:6). If you find you cannot give, you're probably in the wrong church.

Question 4:

What is a tithe, and is it applicable today for Christians?

I've heard it said many times, "The tithe is an Old Testament law, not applicable to the Christian." But I can't confirm that from Scripture. The first tithe in the Bible was given by Abraham 430 years before the Mosaic law was revealed. Hebrews 7:1-10 tells us Abraham tithed to acknowledge God's sovereignty. If the tithe were only an Old Testament law, why then did Abraham tithe 430 years before the law? Abraham tithed as a testimony that God owned everything in his life.

Although the tithe is mentioned in the books of the law, no punishment existed for not tithing. Can you imagine a law with no punishment?

Suppose you run a red light, and a policeman pulls you over and says, "Do you realize that you ran a red light?"

You answer, "Yes."

"Well, okay," he says, "just wanted to let you know."

That would be an ineffective law. Tithing was not a law, but a voluntary act.

The word "tithe" literally means a tenth. Since this is the minimum amount mentioned in the Bible, it would be logical to assume that it's the minimum amount God wants from a believer. If we can't return even the smallest part to God, it merely testifies that the whole has never been surrendered to Him.

In the book of Malachi, the prophet confronted God's people with the fact that they didn't love Him. Yet they said that they did love Him. But the evidence against them was that they didn't give. "Will a man rob God? Yet you are robbing Me! But you say, 'How have we robbed Thee?' In tithes and contributions" (Mal. 3:8). And then in verse 10, God says something through the prophet Malachi that every Christian must hear: "'Bring the whole tithe into the storehouse, so that there may be food in My house, and test Me now in this,' says the Lord of Hosts, 'if I will not open for you the windows of heaven, and pour out for you a blessing until there is no more need.' "

This is the only place in Scripture where God ever told His people to test Him. Plus this passage makes the principle of the tithe clear. It's an outside indicator of an inside spiritual condition. It's our testimony that God owns everything in our lives.

The pastor of a large church did a survey and found out that his church's giving patterns were pretty much average: twenty percent of the people gave eighty percent of the money. Less than thirty percent of them tithed. One Sunday morning, he took the offering plate through the church himself. He opened every envelope and looked at every check. This caused quite a commotion, to say the least.

For the entire week after that service the church was abuzz. Some people were irritated, and everybody wondered what he was up to. The following Sunday he gave a message entitled, "Are you more concerned about what men know than what God knows?" The point was, why be concerned about your pastor knowing how much you give? Why aren't you concerned that God knows?

Question 5:

Our church teaches that the entire tithe should go to the local church. What does Scripture say?

In the book of Malachi we're told that God wants us to direct our entire tithe into the storehouse. So I believe it's necessary that we understand the function of the storehouse in the Old Testament and equate it to our New Testament church.

A storehouse in the Old Testament had four functions: 1) It was used to feed the tribe of Levi and the priests of Aaron. This would seem to be the equivalent of our pastors and staff today. 2) It was used to feed the prophets. A prophet in the Old Testament was not necessarily somebody who could foretell the future but someone who could "forthtell" the truth. In the New Testament church the equivalent would be missionaries and evangelists. 3) It was used to feed the Hebrew widows and orphans living within the city. This would seem to be the equivalent of the widows, orphans, and invalids in our local churches. 4) It was used to feed the widows and orphans of the Gentiles, living in and around the Hebrew city. A special tithe was taken every third year to do this. The equivalent today would be the unsaved people surrounding our local churches.

Many churches in America serve the fourfold function of the Old Testament storehouse, and others do not. Your decision must be based on the church's obedience to God's Word. If a local church doesn't accept the responsibility of being the storehouse, then believers must ensure that the fourfold function is accomplished through other means.

Question 6:

My husband thinks we should tithe on our net income because the taxes that are withheld are not ours to spend; therefore God wouldn't expect us to tithe on the entire amount. My husband also doesn't believe a tithe must be ten percent. I believe it should be ten percent and that we should tithe on the gross income. Who is correct?

Keep in mind what Paul said in 2 Corinthians 9:7, "Let each one do just as he has purposed in his heart; not grudgingly or under compulsion; for God loves a cheerful giver." I don't believe God is concerned with the percentage that we give. However, I do believe that the minimum He ever asked for is a tenth of our income.

According to Proverbs 3:9, we are to honor God from the first fruits of our harvest. I interpret that to mean from the gross. One solution is to pray about this matter together and ask that God lead both of you.

We are also directed in Proverbs 3:5, ". . .Do not lean on your own understanding. In all of your ways acknowledge Him, and He will make your paths straight." I encourage you and your husband to stretch your faith. Whatever you think you can give, give more, and see if God will bless you as a result. As Paul said in 2 Corinthians 9:6, "Now this I say, he who sows sparingly shall also reap sparingly; and he who sows bountifully shall also reap bountifully."

Question 7:

My husband and I both work. Should we tithe from our total income, or just my husband's income, since I don't intend to work for a long period of time?

I believe that you should do whatever God convicts you to do. God's Word says we should tithe on whatever comes into our possession, and in your case that includes both salaries. I also encourage you not to consider any income as "yours" or "his" but "ours." God looks at a married couple as "one" (Gen. 2:24).

Question 8:

I'm a Christian, but my husband is not, and I desire to tithe. My husband doesn't want to. Should I do it anyway? I've had counsel from Christians on both sides of the issue. I want to honor my husband, but should I honor him above the Lord?

First, remember that it's not the money you give that is important, it's your attitude. First Peter 3:1-6 says that a wife is to be submissive, even to her unsaved husband, as she would be to the Lord. Your reward from God comes as a result of your attitude.

When you have committed in your heart to give, your reward from God is assured at that point.

I might also offer a suggestion. Ask your husband if he will allow you to begin giving something. Perhaps it's only fifty dollars per month. Tell him you would like to do this for at least one year. At the end of that year, you'll stop, and together you'll determine if you're better or worse off financially. If you're worse off financially, you'll stop giving. If you're better off, then you would like to give more, until ultimately you're tithing.

Obviously, this is a test of God, but I also believe that God allows us to test Him (Mal. 3:10). Let God prove Himself to your husband. Many wives I have counseled have done this, and found it to be the first step in their husbands coming to the Lord.

Question 9:

I'm a Christian, but my wife isn't. I want to give a tithe, but my wife disagrees and we end up arguing. Do you believe that as a Christian husband, and the authority in my home, I should tithe regardless of whether my wife wants to?

Clearly, according to God's Word, the husband is to be a leader in his home. But I don't believe giving should cause a rift in your marriage. You should make every attempt to share with your wife the biblical principle about tithing, its purpose, and even to challenge her to tithe as a family and see how God blesses the finances.

Ultimately, as the authority over your family, even though your wife doesn't agree, you must tithe if you continue to feel compelled by God to give. It may temporarily alienate her, but most women are looking for strong, godly leadership. If other Christian principles are real in your life, she'll see that tithing is a commitment, not a legalism.

Don't force this decision on your wife merely to assert your authority, however. Try to convince her that it's a heartfelt conviction. Counsel with her and seek her opinion to see if there is a reasonable middle ground. Perhaps you could give a lesser amount for a time. That might show her that you care about her feelings. I believe that God will prove Himself faithful in your finances, but ultimately, the decision is yours. "He who loves father or mother more than Me is not worthy of Me; and he who loves son or daughter more than Me is not worthy of Me" (Matt. 10:37).

Question 10:

Both my wife and I have parents who are in financial need. Neither set has a retirement plan, and both are trying to get by only on Social Security. Can we legitimately use a portion of our tithe to help them? I have asked several Christians. The responses have ranged from a plain "no," to a cold stare, as if I were trying to steal from God. Can you help me?

It's interesting that the Ten Commandments God gave Moses included the admonition to honor your father and mother, but said nothing about giving to God. I find myself in difficulty regardless how I answer this question, either from those who are legalistic and believe the tithe is a commandment, or from those who are libertines and believe that a Christian should never be caught tithing.

Perhaps I can put it in the right scriptural balance. In Matthew 15:5-6, Christ confronted the Pharisees with their hypocrisy, saying, "But you say, 'Whoever shall say to his father or mother, "Anything of mine you might have been helped by has been given to God," he is not to honor his father or his mother.' And thus you invalidate the Word of God for the sake of your tradition."

Christ confronted the Pharisees who were teaching that the Jews couldn't help their parents because their surplus funds had been committed to God and could not be diverted. The Lord said that their parents were as much a part of God's kingdom as the storehouse. If your parents have a need, and you have no additional money with which to help them, they are your first priority. However, I believe you need to be absolutely sure that no other funds are available in your budget. Otherwise, you could be robbing God to maintain your life-style.

Question 11:

Do you think it's proper for us to use part of our tithe to keep our children in a Christian school?

The tithe belongs to God. It's our material testimony that God owns everything in our lives. When you take a portion of your tithe and divert it to keep your children in a Christian school, it's really a gift in self-interest. Educational costs are a normal responsibility of a family. I believe that if you will commit the tithe to God and not use it for your children's school, He will provide a way for them to attend a Christian school, if it's His will.

Question 12:

I give a portion of my income at work to the United Way and other secular organizations. I believe that if these organizations are doing the work that God wants done, they are worthy of receiving a portion of our tithe. My wife disagrees. Can you give us some guidelines?

The tithe is the portion of our income that has been committed to God and is given as a testimony in His name. The ministries that serve in God's name should be recipients of our tithes. Again, it's our testimony that God owns everything, including our finances. The tithe should not be used to support secular organizations. However, that doesn't mean they're not worthy. It's fine to support them, but do it with other money, not your tithe.

Question 13:

We owe a lot of debts from a business failure. Recently I became a Christian, and I've been asking other Christians whether I should tithe while I still owe these large debts. I get mixed answers. What does God expect of me?

A farmer always keeps a portion of each harvest as seed stock to be planted next season. If he didn't, he could never grow another crop. As Christians, our tithes are our seed stock (2 Cor. 9:10). Proverbs 3:9-10 says we are to honor God from the "first fruits." Therefore, the first portion of everything we receive belongs to God. It doesn't belong to anybody else, even a creditor.

I have heard Christians say, "I don't think it honors God to tithe while I still owe a past due debt."

I could accept that argument if they would do just one thing for me. Write the Internal Revenue Service, and say, "I'm sorry but I don't think I should pay taxes while I'm in debt. I'll wait until I get out of debt, and then I'll pay my taxes again."

Why do they pay their taxes? Because they fear the government. Proverbs 1:7 says that the fear of the Lord is the beginning of knowledge.

I have also had creditors call and say, "I don't see why I should take a reduced payment while they're giving to their church."

I simply share with the creditors the principle of the tithe—that it's a commitment to God, not to a church. I also share an observation that those who tithe are almost always better money handlers, and as a result of their commitment to God, they will honor their commitment to their creditors. Rarely does a creditor object after that. In fact, almost everyone respects the commitment, even though most aren't Christians themselves.

God's Word says that, if we tithe, God will give us His wisdom (Deut. 14:23). If there were ever anyone in the world who needs God's wisdom in finances, it is those who are in debt.

Question 14:

Recently I read that the Old Testament tithe was a lot more than ten percent. Is that true?

Actually, three tithes are described in the Old Testament. Two tithes were given each year; every third year, an additional tithe was given for the Gentile widows and orphans living in the Jewish city. The average yearly tithe then was twenty-three and one-third percent. In addition, special offerings, including burnt offerings of animals, sacrifices, contributions, offerings made in honor of vows, freewill offerings, and first-born offerings were also made. Every third year a special offering was taken for the Levites who owned no land. For more information, see Deuteronomy 12:6-7, 14:22-29, 18:1-4, and 26:12.

Question 15:

What is the difference between a pledge and a faith promise? Are they scriptural?

A pledge is a legally enforceable commitment to pay a fixed amount of money during a given period of time. In fact, some churches resell pledges (at a discount) to lending institutions so they can get their money right away. I disagree with that practice, however.

With a faith promise, one makes a commitment to give if the funds are available. In other words, if God provides, you will give. The author of Hebrews says, ". . .Faith is the assurance of things hoped for, the conviction of things not seen" (Heb. 11:1).

I believe a faith promise is scriptural. It allows a church to plan, based on the income that the congregation members have promised if God provides it to them.

I believe a pledge is unscriptural. An absolute commitment without the funds in hand constitutes surety—an obligation to pay without a certain way to pay it.

Question 16:

I have heard many people say we need to give to God to receive from Him. Can God really be pressured to give us something if everything belongs to Him in the first place? This idea sounds a lot like a bribe to me. What do you think?

Perhaps the passage most commonly associated with the "name it, claim it" philosophy is Luke 6:38: "Give, and it will be given to you; good measure, pressed down, shaken together, running over, they will pour into your lap. For whatever measure you deal out to others, it will be dealt to you in return."

I have often heard this Scripture used to make the point that whatever you give to God, God is obligated to multiply it tenfold and give it back. I don't believe that's what Luke 6:38 means. I do believe, however, in the principle of sowing and reaping. In other words, you'll never grow crops if you don't plant seeds.

You are correct, of course, to say that one can't bribe God. Paul says in Romans 11:34-35, "For who has known the mind of the Lord, or became His counselor? Or who has first given to Him that it might be paid back to Him again?" In other words, one can't force God to do anything. God gives to us based on our attitudes.

There is a biblical principle of giving and receiving, but every promise that God makes to us requires an action on our part. Therefore, it's necessary to "believe," or act, to receive God's promises. But those who give, demanding to receive, quickly find out that God is not obligated to do anything. We serve God; He does not serve us.

The spiritual principle behind Luke 6:38 is indeed giving and receiving, but it is not giving to receive. You must go back to Luke 6:27-37 to find what is necessary to start receiving as described in Luke 6:38. These verses describe a life surrendered to God.

Question 17:

Should Christians take tax deductions for contributions to the Lord's work?

Giving to reduce your taxable income is giving in self-interest, and it's the wrong motive. If you doubt your motives, I recommend donating the tax savings back to God also. Then you'll know for sure that your motives are true. There is nothing wrong with taking the income tax deduction as long as that is not the motivation for giving. But every Christian has to honestly ask him or herself, "Would I continue to give even if I didn't get a tax deduction?"

Question 18:

I'm a pastor. Quite often members of our congregation give us junk and then write it off on their income tax. We get worn-out cars, worn-out clothes, and other items that they have no use for. I have a real problem with this. Could you give me some direction?

I often ask Christians who are content to give junk to God—if they would like to get junk back from God. I suspect not. I don't believe that a church should be a refuse dump for unuseable items. My counsel is, if you can't use it, refuse it. Set up a screening committee to evaluate all non-cash gifts. If you don't have an actual use for the item, or it's not readily convertible into cash, don't accept it. Groups like the Salvation Army and Goodwill Industries refurbish used furniture, clothing, appliances, etc., and turn them into assets. Refer your donors to them.

Question 19:

I'm a new Christian and a member of a church that takes an offering at each service. I find myself resentful when the offering plate is passed. It's like the church is begging people to give to God's work. Is it appropriate for churches to do this?

Scripture does not regulate how the offering should be collected. In 1 Corinthians 16:1-2, Paul does direct a local church to collect money. "Now concerning the collection for the saints, as I directed the churches of Galatia, so do you also. On the first day of every week let each one of you put aside and save, as he may prosper, that no collections be made when I come."

The first day of the week was Sunday and that was the normal worship day in the Corinthian church. So Paul was asking them to put aside money on Sunday, very possibly during a church gathering. The passing of a collection plate is a tradition of the modern church. I don't believe any Christian should be offended by this. Don't think of it as a sign of begging, but as a reminder to support God's work. If you have a problem with putting money in the collection plate, then mail a check to the church.

Question 20:

With so many Christian groups asking for money and doing good work, I find it difficult to discern whom to give to. Do you have some guidelines?

First, husband and wife need to seek God's direction together. Then ask the following questions before you give to an organization: 1) Is its message true to God's Word? 2) Are people responding to it, either by accepting Christ or by becoming stronger Christians? 3) Is the organization seeking and accomplishing godly goals? 4) Are the leaders' lives consistent with scriptural principles? 5) Is the organization multiplying itself through others by discipleship? 6) Is there a standard of excellence along with an absence of waste and lavishness in the organization? (When an organization spends more than twenty-five percent of its money raising more money, be cautious.) 7) What do other Christian organizations say about that organization? 8) Do you believe that God is leading you specifically to give to the organization?

Obviously, God doesn't convict every individual to give to every organization. And God will put on the hearts of His people the ministries He wants them to support. Don't give merely because of someone's emotional appeal. It's important to give to those ministries from which you have benefitted. In Galatians 6:6 Paul writes, "And let the one who is taught the word share all good things with him who teaches."

Question 21:

I'm inundated with letters from people begging for money; they

promise me everything from Bibles to prayer cloths if I contribute.
What is the right way to handle these?

I think it's unfortunate that some Christian ministries have gone
to such extremes. Fortunately, they are not a majority, but sometimes they are the most visible.

I recall watching a television program in which an evangelist
bartered promises from God for financial commitments. For $1,000
you had the right to ask God to meet a material need. For $10,000
you had the right to ask God to save one of your loved ones. For
$100,000 you had the right to ask God to heal you.

I wrote this individual a letter confronting him with his deception and asking him to give me specific references in God's Word
in which such promises were made. He never did respond. I think
as Christians we need to hold organizations accountable for how
their money is raised and spent.

Also, remember that if you do receive a premium such as a Bible, a book, or a cassette, you must reduce your charitable deduction by the gift's value.

Question 22:

How can one find out if a Christian organization is using do-
nated money properly? Do donors have the right to ask for infor-
mation? If so, what information should be requested?

You have the right (and responsibility) to know how an organization spends the money you send. If you have doubts, ask for a
copy of its financial statement. If you don't receive one (or if
you're told none is available), be very cautious. Also, you can ask
for a copy of an organization's form 990, which must be filed annually with the Internal Revenue Service. The form describes
where the funds are raised and how they are spent.

Obviously it would cost a great deal of money for a ministry to
send a financial statement to every donor. You should limit this request to organizations to which you give $500 or more a year.

Question 23:

Should I ever contribute directly to a needy person rather than through a church or other Christian organization? What are the advantages and disadvantages of doing this?

Sometimes it's proper to give directly to an individual. For example, when you're trying to teach children the purpose of giving, it's good to have them help a needy family. This allows them to see the benefits of giving in the lives of real people. If they give only through a church offering, your children may miss this.

A second reason is that you also may want to have a personal ministry in people's lives. This is evidence of truly caring, as 1 John 3:17 says: "But whoever has the world's goods, and beholds his brother in need and closes his heart against him, how does the love of God abide in him?" Giving directly to somebody demonstrates that you love and care about that person.

But I would be cautious about giving cash. I suggest instead that you pay for what they need, whether it's utilities, groceries, rent, or clothing. Too often a cash gift is diverted or misused.

I also recommend that before you give to anyone, you verify that their needs are real, and not the result of mismanagement. If you don't know how to provide financial counseling yourself, help them find someone who can. Be certain that what you're doing is helping them out of a problem and not contributing to their problems.

Question 24:

When I'm approached by a beggar I usually give money, but then I wonder whether I did the right thing. What do you think?

I recommend that rather than giving money to someone who approaches you on the street, try to meet the need. If the beggar asks for food, take that person to a restaurant and pay for the meal. This will give you an opportunity to find out who he or she is, and perhaps to share your faith.

If you don't have the time to get involved, pass by. Don't give money. More often than not, you're just contributing to a drinking or drug problem. "For even when we were with you, we used to give you this order: If anyone will not work, neither let him eat" (2 Thess. 3:30).

Question 25:

How do you handle organizations that solicit funds door-to-door or on street corners? Quite often the solicitors are teenagers. It seems unfair that they put abnormal pressures on us. People also solicit money in shopping malls and store entrances. Sometimes the organizations sound Christian. Should Christians give to them?

I would counsel any Christian to be careful about giving money to people who solicit door-to-door, in malls, or in airports. Some of these organizations are cults. I would never give to an organization until I learned what it stood for (and how it uses its money). If you're not careful, your dollar may help a guru buy another limo.

If an organization sounds interesting to you, take the time to get the headquarters' address and write for more information, including a financial statement.

Question 26:

I disagree with how our church denomination spends money, and so I designate my tithe to be used locally and not sent to denominational headquarters. Is it proper for me to do this?

Before answering the question, first let me say that, if you disagree with the denomination, you need to express your disagreements. Go to the pastor, voice your concerns, and get his permission to also discuss your objections with the denominational leadership. You not only have the right but also a responsibility to verify that your funds are not used for unscriptural purposes. I know of no scriptural principle that would keep you from excluding the denomination from your giving, if you feel the necessity.

Question 27:

I have a Christian friend in need, but if I give him money, I'm quite sure he will misspend it. Should I direct how the money can be spent? Would I be better off giving or lending it to him?

If you really want to help your friend, see that he gets some financial counseling. Generally, I would recommend that you lend him the money, rather than give it to him. I suggest lending not so you can get your money back, but because that will help your friend establish financial discipline.

Under the supervision of a financial counselor, set up a repayment schedule (without interest), but require that he make regular payments. You should be willing to forfeit the money if it's not repaid, so don't lend what you can't afford to lose.

Question 28:

My church doesn't really want to be bothered with receiving such things as real estate, stocks, and bonds. My pastor asks that we sell them ourselves and just give the money. Aren't there some advantages to giving appreciated properties as opposed to cash?

Yes, I've found that giving appreciated properties is excellent stewardship. Under our tax system, if you sell an appreciated property, you're going to be taxed on the profit. If you give the property prior to sale, you can avoid virtually all the taxes and still get a tax deduction for the property's value.

For example, let's assume you want to make a gift to your church, and you have a stock that you bought for $100 that is now worth $200. If you sell the stock, you're going to be taxed on the one hundred dollar gain.

If you give the entire two hundred dollars sale price to the church, no tax is to be paid (except possibly Social Security tax). So, the church gets $200, and you're not taxed.

Now, let's assume you give the stock directly to your church. The church can sell the stock and not have to pay tax, since it is a nontaxed organization. You're still able to deduct $200 for the gift. Assuming you were in a twenty-five percent tax bracket, you would get $50 back in taxes that could be given to your church.

I believe this is a tremendous method to give more to the church and avoid the tax consequences. This also applies to other appreciated assets, such as land and buildings. But one caution: Be sure you're giving assets that are valuable and can easily be converted into cash.

Question 29:

We give to an organization that sends gifts such as books or tapes in exchange for donations. Can I deduct from my taxes the full amount of my check, or must I subtract the value of the book or tape?

As of this writing, you're required to deduct the fair market value of the premium from your cash donation. Some organizations do not make that clear, but it's the responsibility of the donor to reduce his or her gift by the value of the premium.

Question 30:

I'm a member of a dynamic church, and we're committed to serving God and God's people. One of the biggest flaws in our church, however, is the lack of help to people with financial problems. How do we set up a church benevolence program and how would we operate it scripturally?

In 2 Corinthians 9:13, the Apostle Paul wrote, "Because of the proof given by this ministry they will glorify God for your obedience to your confession of the gospel of Christ, and for the liberality of your contribution to them and to all." Scripturally, benevolence is not an option for the local church; it's an absolute responsibility. It's not the government's responsibility to administer welfare to Christians; it's the responsibility of Christians in the local church.

As you begin a ministry of benevolence, you should establish written standards for those you're going to help. Who will you assist, under what conditions, and how much will you provide? People should be screened by a benevolence committee and should be individually counseled by a trained financial counselor within the church before funds are given. The emphasis should be on helping them solve their problems. In most cases, those problems were brought on by the lack of discipline or self-control, although this isn't always true.

Benevolence is an essential and required part of God's plan for the local church. It should be done in a disciplined fashion to ensure that the church is really helping people who have legitimate needs. Those who are undisciplined must be disciplined in God's principles of finances. "And one of you says to them, 'Go in peace, be warmed and be filled'; and yet you do not give them what is necessary for their body; what use is that? Even so faith, if it has no works, is dead, being by itself" (James 2:16-17).

CHAPTER 8

Inheritance and Wills

Question 1:   *Should parents leave an inheritance for their children?*

Question 2:   *Must I leave equal amounts to all children?*

Question 3:   *Would a letter of my intent substitute for a will?*

Question 4:   *If a will is drawn up without an attorney, is it any good?*

Question 5:   *How can we leave money to our church and to missionaries as well as to our children?*

Question 6:   *Should we leave money to non-Christian children?*

Question 7:   *How can I transfer assets now but use them while I'm living?*

Question 8:   *Doesn't my spouse automatically get my assets if I die?*

Question 9:   *Should I disinherit my daughter, who is in a cult?*

Almost eighty percent of all American adults have no valid will. If they died, they would leave the distribution of their estates and guardianship of their children to the state. Nobody ever thinks he or she will die prematurely, yet the average age at which a woman is widowed (eighty-five percent of men die first) in the United States is fifty-two.

Many Christian couples have difficult decisions facing them as they consider leaving an inheritance to non-Christian children or to irresponsible children. More and more families are having to face the "his and hers" children issue and how to be fair in second-marriage situations.

An even more fundamental biblical issue is whether a parent has an obligation to leave an inheritance to children. If so, how large, and when should it be given?

"When there is a man who has labored with wisdom, knowledge and skill, then he gives his legacy to one who has not labored with them. This too is vanity and a great evil" (Eccl. 2:21).

Question 1:

Should we, as Christian parents, leave an inheritance for our children? What are some guidelines?

I believe that inheritance is proper. Generally in the Bible, it was given to adult children before the parent died. According to Jewish tradition, a father would begin to pass along his inheritance to his oldest son when he reached his mid-thirties. Eventually, he inherited most of the property that his father was going to give him while the father was still around to show him how to manage it.

This example is found in the parable of the prodigal son (Luke 15:11-24). The number-two son came to his father and asked for his inheritance, and the father gave it. As number-two sons are prone to do, he traveled off to a foreign land and squandered all the money. Then, when he came back, his father was still alive and able to give him direction.

In Ecclesiastes 6:3, Solomon wrote, "If a man fathers a

hundred children and lives many years, however many they be, but his soul is not satisfied with good things, and he does not even have a proper burial, then I say, 'Better the miscarriage than he.' " This man didn't accumulate enough to even get a proper burial, let alone provide for his children.

The principle of inheritance is scriptural. The problem is that most parents wait until death and then have no opportunity to oversee the inheritance's use. Whatever you want to give to your children, give it while you're living, if at all possible. There's an old cliche, "Do your giving while you're living, so you're knowing where it's going." Remember that inheritance is not only material, it's also spiritual.

Question 2:

Am I to give more inheritance to my oldest child than to younger children? Am I to give to unsaved children?

First, it's important to understand the biblical principles behind inheritance. We know that it's the parents' responsibility to store up for their children. As Paul says, "Here for this third time I am ready to come to you, and I will not be a burden to you; for I do not seek what is yours, but you; for children are not responsible to save up for their parents, but parents for their children" (2 Cor. 12:14). While Paul is referring to spiritual values in this passage, I also believe he is referring to finances, since that is a major theme of Second Corinthians.

Each and every couple has to decide how much to leave, based on God's plan for their lives. Scripture really leaves the choices to the parents. You need to evaluate both the management abilities and the financial needs of your children to decide how the assets should be allocated.

An inheritance is meant to be a "living gift," meaning that it's given prior to death, unless a parent suffers an untimely death. But regardless of when your children receive their inheritance, I would encourage you not to give them their entire inheritance at one time, particularly at an early age. It would be better to give it to them in successive portions, perhaps beginning at age twenty-five through age thirty-five or forty. That way the errors of youth should be overcome.

Regarding the distribution of your assets to unsaved children, that also is an issue that each couple must determine. I can find no scriptural principle that directs a believer to exclude an unsaved child from his or her rightful portion of an inheritance, provided that child isn't anti-Christian (such as involved in a cult). What that portion is exactly, is up to the couple and God. Because it's all God's property, we as God's stewards must be careful to distribute those assets according to God's wishes and desires rather than our own.

Question 3:

My wife and I don't have many assets. It seems the cost of drawing up a will is high compared to the benefits. Can't we just write a letter describing how things should be divided up and leave it at that?

It's quite possible that your letter will not suffice as a will. If you don't have a will that is probational (provable) in court according to your state's law, then when you die, the state will decide how your assets will be distributed. This is known as dying "intestate" (no after-death bequest). The state will distribute your assets and designate your children's guardians if both you and your wife die. The children will normally go to the nearest living relatives, regardless of whether they share your values. Please accept your responsibility and have wills drawn up by a competent attorney. Remember, both husband and wife should have wills. In most areas, a will costs less than two hundred dollars.

I'm mindful of Proverbs 22:3: "The prudent sees the evil and hides himself, but the naive go on, and are punished for it." I have helped many widows whose husbands died without wills. I can tell you, it's a very costly and lengthy process to get the assets distributed properly.

In the mid 1970s I counseled three Christian widows whose husbands died in the same airplane crash. All three had been through our counseling and had planned to have wills drawn, but only one had actually done so. Within three months, his estate was settled, the insurance proceeds securely invested, and the family re-settled near the grandparents. The total legal bills amounted to less than $1,000.

The other two dragged on for years, with one of the women ultimately receiving a child's share of her husband's estate. One of the families contested its settlement, and it took nearly seven years and $25,000 to resolve what a $200 will would have settled in thirty days.

By the way, both of these husbands thought they didn't have estates large enough to worry about. The final insurance settlement from the crash was over one million dollars apiece. It was more than enough to make a remote family member turn up and fight for his or her "share."

Question 4:

If we draw up our own will in the presence of witnesses, but without an attorney, is it legally binding?

Technically yes, but I have counseled enough widows to know that if you don't do it properly, it is not probational (provable) in court. I suggest that you consult an attorney. A dentist friend of mine drafted his own will but failed to get the correct number of witnesses. He died six years ago, and his estate is still not settled.

Question 5:

We would like to leave money to our church and to some mis-sionaries we support, as well as to our children. What is the best way to do this?

You can name any beneficiaries that you desire. I suggest that if you name charitable organizations, you specify either a percentage or dollar amount to be given. This money will be removed from the value of your estate for estate tax purposes. Then your estate will not be taxed on the portion going to God's work.

Question 6:

My wife and I are Christians, but none of our children are. We've been entrusted by God with a large amount of money. I don't feel good about leaving it to the children, since we have not communicated for a long time, and they're not following God's path. Would it be wise to leave my money to them? What does Scripture say?

Scripture is clear. As long as your children are under your care, you have a responsibility to support them. However, if they no longer are dependent on you, then the assets are yours to do with as you believe God leads. If you don't want to leave anything to your children, you don't have to.

I would, however, counsel you to pray about this, talk it over with your wife, and be absolutely sure this is God's direction. Don't use your assets to "get even" with your children. It may be that by leaving them something, you would have one last opportunity to share the message of salvation with them. Another alternative is to leave something in trust that would be paid out later under very specific and controlled conditions.

Question 7:

I'm a widow whose husband died many years ago. Our children are grown, and over the years I've given most of our assets to them. They've managed things well, and I don't feel that they have any further needs. I would like to ensure that my remaining assets go to the Lord's work, but I need them to live on until I die. How can I accomplish this?

You can place all of your assets in a living trust, with the charitable organizations you want to support as the beneficiaries. You can even place your home into this trust under what is called a "life estate," in which you give up ownership but retain the privilege of living there during your lifetime. At your death, all assets in trust will go immediately to the charitable organizations according to the terms you decided on, and the assets will not be taxed. Because this is a very specialized estate planning law, I encourage you to contact a good Christian attorney in your area to have him handle the entire estate plan for you.

Question 8:

I understand that as long as our properties are jointly owned, my wife and I do not require wills. The properties will revert to the survivor when one of us dies. Is this correct?

If all of your property is held in joint ownership and one of you dies, ownership does revert to the survivor. Depending on the size of your estate, however, there can be significant estate taxes that can only be avoided through good estate planning.

If you were both killed in an accident, for example, then one of you would have died intestate, that is, without a will. All jointly owned assets would be settled by the state, perhaps not to your liking. Please invest the little bit of time and money necessary to get a will for both you and your wife.

Question 9:

Our only daughter is in a cult, and it breaks our hearts. We have considerable assets to leave, but my wife and I question whether we should leave them to her. We know the money ultimately would go to the cult. Do you have some counsel?

Remember that the money you have is not yours; it belongs to God. You are only the stewards of it, and you must use the Lord's money wisely. Would He want it to go to a cult that is leading people away from Him? Tell your daughter why you can't include her in your will. If necessary, put the funds in a trust, with the stipulation that she can't have access to them as long as she's involved with the cult. Then select a trustee whom you trust and give him or her the power to determine distribution. You may alienate your daughter, but take comfort in what the Lord says in Matthew 10:37: "He who loves father or mother more than Me is not worthy of Me; and he who loves son or daughter more than Me is not worthy of Me."

Assure your daughter you still love her and that you pray daily for her. If you're committed to this plan of action because of the Lord, I believe that eventually her resentment will be replaced with respect, as she witnesses your faithfulness to put the Lord first in all things.

CHAPTER 9

Investment and Savings

Question 18: Should a Christian trade commodities?

Question 19: Are gold and silver good investments?

Question 20: Should I invest in no-money-down real estate?

Question 21: What about pyramid sales schemes?

Question 22: Is gambling wrong?

Question 23: Should I enter sweepstakes?

In every question-and-answer session I've ever conducted, the topic that generates the most discussion is investments. Virtually everyone wants to know how to make the most money with the least risk. But for Christians, the question should not be where to invest, or how to invest, but why to invest. Should Christians speculate with money, or does God direct us to give our surplus to the needy? Which investments are compatible with Christian principles and which are a compromise? Does speculation in the stock or commodities markets constitute gambling? This chapter will focus on such questions.

Another issue that will arise in this chapter is the wife's role in investment decisions. Few Christian couples practice the principle of oneness that God's Word prescribes. Consequently, they don't utilize all the wisdom that is available to them. I trust that you will make a commitment to work together on long-range financial goals.

"There is precious treasure and oil in the dwelling of the wise, but a foolish man swallows it up" (Prov. 21:20).

Question 1:

I believe Christians should not invest money. Not only does the practice promote greed, but sometimes money is lost that could have been put to use in God's kingdom. Can you give scriptural justification for investing, rather than donating money immediately?

Yes, I believe so. First, if Christians are already giving what they believe they should, and a surplus remains, then Scripture indicates that it should be put aside for future needs. Proverbs 6:6-11 tells us that the ant stores during the summer, knowing that a time will come when she will need the resources.

If that were all God's Word said about storing, most of the rich would be right on target. However, the balance to the "make all you can, and can all you make" philosophy is found in Luke 12:16-21, the parable of the rich fool. This rich man had an exceptionally large harvest and didn't have room to store it, so he decided to tear down his barns, build larger ones to hoard his surplus, and then quit work to enjoy life.

Somewhere between the careful ant and the foolish hoarder is the balance required of God's steward. God wants us to have some surplus but not an attitude of selfishness or greed. Good management of any surplus requires that some of it be reinvested. The scriptural justification for investing is to provide for future needs by multiplying our surplus. Some legitimate future needs include: 1) the education of your children; 2) the goal of becoming debt free; 3) retirement (within reason); and 4) spontaneous giving as needs are brought to your attention.

While investing is not scripturally wrong, many times the motive behind investing is. Many people today (Christians included) are consumed by fear of the future, greed, covetousness, indulgence, and pride. Many of the "investments" that people lose money in are really get-rich-quick schemes designed to ensnare ignorant speculators. God's main concern is motive. It's not so much what you're investing in, but why you're investing.

The best way to guard against the sin of greed is found in Romans 13:14, "But put on the Lord Jesus Christ, and make no provision for the flesh in regard to its lusts." In other words, check your motives, husband and wife together.

Question 2:

Recently I have begun to realize that some of the mutual fund companies I have invested in engage in questionable and even objectionable activities. I feel responsible as a Christian to do something about this. Do you know of any investments that Christians can safely invest in?

In Colossians 3:17, the Apostle Paul wrote, "And whatever you do in word or deed, do all in the name of the Lord Jesus, giving thanks through Him to God the Father." Because everything we do witnesses to what we believe, some investments will be unacceptable to us.

All Christians should thoroughly check into how their money is being used. If you're investing in a company, get a copy of its prospectus, which reveals how the company's income is generated. If you're investing in mutual funds or something equivalent, get a prospectus disclosing what companies the fund invests in. If you see questionable companies on the list, write them directly and ask for further details. I have done that and found some funds were investing in such activities as abortion and pornographic literature.

Obviously, you can't determine how a company uses every single dollar. Many are conglomerates and are linked to a variety of other companies. The most you can do is verify whether the company is using any visible proportion of its resources to support anti-Christian causes.

Question 3:

I've been investing in the stock market for several years now. In all honesty, I probably lost as much as I've gained, so I'm about even. But after reading some of your material, my wife thinks the stock market is gambling, and I should get out. Do you agree?

Proverbs 23:4-5 warns us against the wrong attitude toward worldly riches. I believe most stock market investors should heed that proverb. I suspect most have a get-rich-quick attitude, believing that they can gain something for virtually nothing. If that's a person's attitude, then the stock market constitutes gambling.

Of course, to some extent any stock investment is a gamble. If you put money into a company's stock, you're taking a chance, that is, a gamble. If the stock goes up, you make money. If it goes down, you lose money. In the same way, you gamble on the roulette wheel. If the little ball falls on your number, you win. If it doesn't, you lose.

But you can lower the stock market risk by understanding economics and the industries in which you're investing. So the stock market does have a legitimate function just as the commodities market does. The stock market provides equity capital to businesses so they don't have to borrow. Speculation takes place when investors decide to trade a company's stock.

Question 4:

I have some money that I need to put into a retirement plan. An insurance salesman from my church told me that an annuity is a good investment. Could you give me a little information about annuities?

First, a point about retirement funds. If you're putting funds aside for retirement, I recommend that they be placed where you can't get to them too easily. An annuity accomplishes this because of the penalties attached to early withdrawal. If you're going to put money into an annuity, I recommend that you read all you can about it. Many varieties exist, but there are really only two basic types, fixed and variable.

With a fixed annuity, you pay into the fund for a given number of years. At retirement, it begins to pay back a fixed amount of money each month. The amount you receive does not vary, regardless of economic conditions.

A variable annuity also requires regular payments prior to retirement. But at retirement, it pays back based on the actual earnings of the fund.

The benefit of a fixed annuity usually falls to those approaching retirement, who need to depend on a fixed amount of money each month. The variable annuity is usually more beneficial to younger people, who can't project what their money will be worth at retirement. Therefore, they don't want to get locked into a fixed income. They hedge their investments by basing their future incomes on annuities' earnings. Over the last twenty years, annuities have become popular investments for retirement planning.

Question 5:

My wife and I have been contributing to an IRA for several years. Although the 1986 Tax Reform Act prevents us from deducting our IRA contributions because the investment accumulates tax free, I still think it's a great benefit. Do you agree?

For those people who can deduct the contribution to an IRA from their income, it's an excellent tax shelter. For example, if you are in a twenty-five percent income tax bracket and you invest in an IRA, in effect you earned at least twenty-five percent that first year because of tax savings.

Also, IRAs have gained additional flexibility in the last few years because you now can select your own investments. In my opinion, one of the best places to invest IRA money is in good quality mutual funds. Some of the better funds have earned in excess of twenty percent per year for several years.

Regarding an IRA in which the initial investment is not tax deductible, the benefit is obviously reduced. However, since the earnings on the funds within an IRA are still tax deferred, it's a good long-range method to save money.

The concept of self-help at retirement is a good one, and IRAs contribute to that. Although ours is the most affluent society in the world, we save comparatively little. God's Word says savings is a good habit and discipline to develop (Prov. 30:25-26).

Question 6:

I would like to find an investment counselor. I'm hesitant to approach somebody in my church because I don't want anyone there to know exactly how much money I have. Also, it seems that every time I used the advice of a Christian, I lost money. Can you tell me how I might find a good counselor?

First, I would suggest you find someone of like mind and attitude. As a Christian, that means you should find an investment counselor who is also a committed Christian.

God's Word offers guidelines for seeking and selecting good counsel. Psalm 1:1 says that we are to avoid ungodly counsel. Proverbs 13:20 suggests we look for wise counsel. (The test of a wise counselor is whether that person makes you more money than he or she costs you.) Proverbs 15:22 points out that we are to have multiple counselors. In other words, don't rely exclusively on the counsel of one individual to make your decisions.

Second, when you have found a prospective counselor, test his or her knowledge. Pick an investment about which you are knowledgeable and ask the counselor some questions about it. Read up ahead of time, if you need to. If you aren't impressed by the answers, look elsewhere for counsel. If the counsel runs contrary to God's Word, discount it as worthless.

Third, test the counselor's value system. Let me give you an old, helpful axiom: "If somebody will cheat for you, he will eventually cheat you." If you find that he or she is willing to bend the rules on your behalf against somebody else, then you can be certain that that counselor will do the same thing to you.

Fourth, verify his or her track record. Proverbs 21:5 says, "The plans of the diligent lead surely to advantage. . . ." Never use a financial counselor who doesn't have at least five years of experience. Ten years would be better. Otherwise, you should assume that you're that person's on-the-job training. Everybody needs that training, but I'd rather an investment counselor get it with someone else's money.

I encourage you to thoroughly check his or her references. Many times people give references but assume you'll never check them. If necessary, ask the references for other references.

A good financial planner should probably be a Certified Financial Planner (CFP), and a Registered Investment Advisor (RIA). These titles attest to his or her acquired knowledge, but not necessarily to the application of it. That person's win-loss record attests to his or her ability.

I recommend that both husband and wife undertake this search. Quite often, God gives a sensitivity and discernment to the wife that her husband doesn't have. She may be able to evaluate not only the counselor's track record but also his or her temperament and spirit.

Question 7:

My wife and I would like to begin investing, but we find it difficult to generate the money to do so. Can you help us?

Saving is always a matter of personal discipline. I once counseled a pastor who had saved more than $250,000 during his forty years in the ministry. And yet, the highest salary he had ever earned was $10,000 a year.

I asked him, "Pastor, if you were to give counsel to a young couple today on how to develop a surplus of money, what would it be?"

"It's simple," he said. "Always spend less than you make."

The issue is really one of self-control, which the Bible says is a "fruit of the spirit" (Gal. 5:23). Developing a surplus is not difficult. All it requires is a little bit of money saved over a long period of time and then used wisely, according to God's principles.

Question 8:

We would like to invest, but we're not certain where to draw the line between our desire to save and to hoard. Is there a difference, and where does one draw the line?

There is a distinct difference between saving and hoarding. Proverbs 6:6-8, the parable of the ant, reads, "Go to the ant, 0 sluggard, observe her ways and be wise, which, having no chief, officer or ruler, prepares her food in the summer, and gathers her provision in the harvest." During the harvest months, an ant gathers the food she will need during the winter months. She puts aside only what she'll need.

I recall an article I read in which an anthill was moved from New England to Florida. During the first year the ants steadily transported and stored food in their chambers. But winter never came, so the next year they cut back on the amount of food they stored. After winter didn't come again the third year, the ants quit storing food. Their supply matched their need.

Saving is good stewardship, a hedge against future needs. Hoarding is a lack of trust. Basically, the difference is attitude.

Over the years, I have counseled many couples who were undergoing financial difficulties because of job losses. Many of these couples actually had savings accounts, but they were borrowing money to live on instead of using their savings. When I asked why, they said they didn't want to use their savings because they needed the security. They would rather go into debt than spend their savings. In reality, they were not saving; they were hoarding.

The thoughtless accumulation of money can become consuming greed and pride. During the Great Depression, Bernard Baruche accumulated billions of dollars.

A reporter once asked him, "Mr. Baruche, I know you're a very wealthy man. How much is going to be enough?"

He said, "Just a little more."

That attitude runs contrary to God's Word, and Christians need to guard against it. What a shame to invest a whole lifetime pursuing worthless goals. "If therefore you have not been faithful in the use of unrighteous Mammon, who will entrust the true riches to you? And if you have not been faithful in the use of that which is another's, who will give you that which is your own?" (Luke 16:11-12).

Make some specific guidelines about how much you need to save and why. Then stick to your plans and don't allow yourself to get caught up in the attitude of the world.

Question 9:

We're working on a budget to get ourselves out of debt. We're also working out a repayment schedule with our creditors. Do we have the right to save while we still owe money to someone else?

I believe that every family should allocate a percentage of its income to savings. If you don't have any savings and your car breaks down, or the washing machine goes out, or the refrigerator quits, then you'll have to rely on credit and ultimately end up deeper in debt.

Many times I have had couples contact their creditors about negotiating lower monthly payments. Often when a creditor reviewed their budgets, which included money set aside for savings, the creditor would call me to ask why he or she should take reduced payments while the couple had savings.

I would always respond, "Because they have made a commitment to no more debt. As long as they don't generate any more debt, you can be assured that they will pay what they have promised."

I rarely had a creditor object further. In reality, if you don't save, you'll probably have to borrow again.

Question 10:

I know that some investments are risky and others are relatively safe. What should my strategy be as I consider investing my savings?

First, you must establish the average amount of money you'll need for emergencies. This might be anywhere from $1,000 to $5,000, depending on your family's needs. These funds should be placed in an insured savings account. Beyond that, your first investment strategy is to eliminate any consumer debt, including auto loans. Once that is accomplished, then you can develop an investment plan.

The most common investment strategy is to maximize your income while minimizing your risks. If all of your assets are left in cash accounts, such as certificates of deposit or treasury bills, you will minimize the risk, but you also minimize your income. If we have an inflationary economy, your assets will lose value. If all your assets are in speculative areas like gold or silver, then you may maximize your profits, but you also maximize the risk.

I believe a good investment strategy is to balance the risks and return. Diversify your investments and take only the risks that are proportionate and reasonable for your age, your income, and the goals that you're trying to reach.

Obviously, it's impossible to cover this subject thoroughly in a brief answer. I would encourage you to write for my free brochure, "10 Keys to Investing," if you need more information. (Write to:

Christian Financial Concepts; P.O. Box 130, Cumming, GA 30130.)

Question 11:

We have $5,000 saved for household contingencies. We want it to be absolutely safe and available when we need it, and we want it to earn interest. What would you recommend for us?

I would suggest that you save your money in an insured account with a bank, savings and loan, or credit union. I would also suggest that you call around and find out who offers the best rate on savings accounts. Banks, savings and loans, and credit unions often compete for these funds, and one may offer as much as one percent higher earnings than the others.

Another good place to keep your savings is a money fund offered by a major stock brokerage company. A money fund is actually a specialized savings account that pays interest and gives you the right to withdraw funds without penalty, but with some withdrawal restriction. Just remember the rule of investing: risk versus return. If you want minimum risk, you also opt for minimum return.

Question 12:

Could you discuss what a money market account is? My son says that I should keep my money in a money market rather than a passbook savings. Are money markets safe?

A money market account (or fund) is an interest-bearing account in which many people pool their money, which is then managed by a professional investment group. Money market accounts are among the highest-earning interest accounts that you can get and still have your money available "on demand." Depending on the particular account, it may or may not be protected by insurance.

In general, a money market account is an "at risk" investment, not a guaranteed savings account. The value of your shares in the account depends on the total value of the investments owned by the account at any given time. If your money is invested in an uninsured account and you feel that you can't afford to risk losing your funds, I would suggest that you move it to an insured fund.

Usually the major brokerage firms which offer these accounts also offer government funds, meaning that your money is backed by U.S. government securities. You need to be very careful because some of these funds don't actually own the government securities. They buy "repurchase agreements," meaning that the actual government securities are owned by another institution that has pledged them as collateral. Therefore, you are actually lending the money to that institution and not to the government. The best way to know this is to ask your salesman or broker.

Question 13:

I am a recent widow, and I have just received my husband's insurance proceeds. My accountant recommended that I place it in a CD. Could you explain what a CD is?

A certificate of deposit (CD) is an interest-bearing note issued by a bank. These are time-related notes that mature (become payable) according to your contractual agreement with the bank. The time period can vary from thirty days to ten years. Generally, the longer the maturation period, the higher the interest paid. Early withdrawal results in substantial interest forfeiture.

CD's are insured up to $100,000 per depositor if the issuing bank is a member of the Federal Depositors' Insurance Corporation (FDIC). Those issued by a Savings and Loan should be insured by the Federal Savings and Loan Insurance Corporation (FSLIC).

Question 14:

Could you explain what a mutual fund is? My company has been investing our retirement funds in one for several years now.

A mutual fund is an investment in which individuals can pool their money to purchase different kinds of securities, such as stocks and bonds. Mutual funds in general are good investment vehicles for the low-budget investor because they provide diversification and professional management. Some mutual funds invest in aggressive growth companies, while others invest in more stable "blue chip" stocks. Because they are investments, you can lose money as well as make it. Select your fund based on cost, risk, and track record.

Mutual funds operate to make a profit, first for the managing company and then for you, the investor. The company and salesmen make their money through a fee system. There are two kinds of fees structures: front-load and no-load. Front-load mutual funds charge a fee when you buy your shares, so your initial investment is reduced by the amount of the fee. "No-load" means that rather than charging you up front, the fee is amortized over a number of years. In theory, a no-load fund should have higher earnings because more of your money is working for you. Practically speaking, there is little difference between the two.

Many mutual fund companies offer investors the flexibility of shifting their investments among different funds in their "family" of funds. Thus, you can shift from growth stocks to blue chip stocks, or from stocks to bonds, or even to a money market account, where your funds are held in cash.

This is a helpful option. If interest rates are high, and stock prices are low, you would want to shift to an interest-bearing account. Then, when stock prices cycle up, you would shift to a good stock fund. Most good business magazines regularly assess the track records of mutual funds. Consult them for selections.

Question 15:

I'm thinking about investing in rental housing. What cautions do you have?

In my opinion, rental housing is one of the better investments for the average family, primarily because most families are familiar with how to select and maintain a home. The better you understand an investment, generally speaking, the better it will pay off for you.

Advantages to rental housing as an investment include: 1) You can depreciate the house and write off that depreciation against income from the house. 2) The rental payments are actually retiring the mortgage on the house. 3) Rental housing has been relatively inflation proof and can become a good retirement income supplement. 4) You can employ your children to do some of the work such as lawn care, painting, rent collections, etc. and teach them about business and work ethics.

Some distinct disadvantages with rental housing also exist. The biggest is being a landlord. There is nothing more irritating than getting a 2 a.m. call from a tenant who says his or her plumbing is stopped up. Also, you must have the temperament to be a landlord. It's not easy for anyone, and it's impossible for some.

In addition, you can get caught in a cyclical economy where your rental house is vacant, and you'll have to carry the payments. If your budget won't accommodate this, I recommend you avoid rental housing.

Question 16:

When we were on vacation in Florida last year, my wife and I bought into a time-share condominium. We have the right to use the condo two weeks a year or to rent it to others. Having heard some of your negative comments about these, can you clarify the problems for me?

The first problem with a time-share condominium is that many times buyers pay too much. It's not uncommon to pay $200 to $250 per square foot for a time-share when you could buy a similar unit for less than $100 per square foot outright.

Second, rarely do most couples go back to the same place for vacations every year. Although many sales groups offer buyers the right to trade their time-share in one location for one somewhere else, most people find that it's very difficult to do.

If you don't use your time-share, many sales groups also offer to rent it for you. But unless you have the ideal time, such as tourist season in Florida, you'll find that renters are scarce.

I've found that most people who purchase a time-share condominium do so on impulse and later discover it was an expensive indulgence. Usually they buy while on vacation because it's the one time of the year when they feel relaxed, and they want to re-create the feeling each year. The time-share sales groups understand this mentality very well and capitalize on it.

Very few of the couples I counsel actually used their time-share for vacation after the first year or two. They put it up for rent but found that they have very few renters. Almost always a time-share contract contains a contingent liability in the form of an annual maintenance fee that must be paid for as long as you own the unit.

Remember, most purchases such as these are impulse decisions. Bear in mind what Proverbs 21:5 says, "The plans of the diligent lead surely to advantage, but everyone who is hasty comes surely to poverty."

Question 17:

I've been thinking about investing in art, and perhaps in antique rugs and antique furniture, or other such items that we can use while they are appreciating. Could you give me some ideas about the best way to get started? What do you think about collectibles as investments?

If you take the time to learn exactly what you're doing, collectibles can be excellent investments. However, success or failure really depends on your individual expertise. One of the best ways to acquire the knowledge you need is to subscribe to magazines or books that specialize in the particular collectible that interests you. When you feel you have gained enough insight, take a small amount of money and invest on a limited scale.

A word of caution: Decide in the beginning whether you're making purchases or investments. If you're investing in collectibles, don't use them in your home. It's easy to get attached to something and then not be willing to resell it, even at a profit.

A friend once told me he was going to buy his wife an investment-grade diamond and have it made into a ring. "So she can enjoy it while it's appreciating," he said.

I replied, "You just made a purchase, not an investment. The only way you'll ever get that ring off is with a hatchet."

Question 18:

I'm a broker in the commodities market. I have two questions. First, should a Christian do this kind of work? Second, as a seller of commodities in which seventy-five percent of the buyers lose money, am I preying on other people's ignorance?

For most commodities speculators, there's no risk to it. They always lose. As a professional broker, your risk is reduced by accumulated knowledge. This may well be God's plan for your life. However, for most laymen, it's one of the best ways to lose a lot of money—fast. In fact, for the amateur, it's as much gambling as playing a roulette wheel, maybe even more so, because the odds in the commodities market for the nonprofessional are much higher than on a roulette wheel. Proverbs 21:5 tells us that a man who hastens to get wealthy fast will get poor even quicker.

The commodities market serves a legitimate function. It provides the farmer an opportunity to presell his crop so that he knows what his profit is going to be. But whenever people begin to trade in commodities without any intention of taking delivery of any product, it becomes pure speculation. This is the case with the majority of all commodities trading.

A speculator purchases a contract for future delivery of a commodity at a specified price but actually never intends to receive the product. If the price he or she has agreed to pay is less than the product's market price when the contract matures, he or she sells the contract and reaps a profit. But if the market price drops substantially, that person sells the contract and takes a loss.

Since many futures contracts are sold "on margin" (financed), the losses can be substantial. One doctor I counseled bought $500,000 worth of soybean contracts on margin ($50,000 down). The price of soybeans dropped steadily until he sold out for $200,000. His loss was $300,000, or 600 percent on his investment.

Question 19:

How do you feel about gold and silver as investments?

I believe Christians can invest in any area provided they know the potential risk and return and don't risk money they can't afford to lose. Gold has been used as a standard of value worldwide for thousands of years because: 1) it's easily storable; 2) it's divisible into small pieces; and 3) it's a limited resource that can't be counterfeited. Silver, to a lesser degree, serves the same function.

I believe that buying gold and silver as a hedge against runaway inflation or a financial collapse does make some sense. However, the majority of people who buy gold or silver do so because it's a speculative commodity. They buy it at one price, hoping to sell it at a higher price. Gold and silver prices rise and fall with cycles in the economy, and very few people are able to accurately forecast these cycles. In my opinion, gold and silver are not good short-term investments for the average investor. A good quality mutual fund with professional advisors specializing in gold or silver would be better diversification.

Question 20:

What is your opinion of no-money-down real estate investments?

If you have been following the no-money-down real estate philosophy, you know its advocates make their money by selling books. Many people I have counseled tried it and lost everything.

Most people lose at this game for one of two reasons. First, the properties are often poorly located and poorly maintained. The best buys in no-money-down houses are in depressed areas of the country. They're available because they can't be rented at a profitable rate to reliable tenants. People who are enticed to buy them for no money down often find that they can't rent them either, and they end up borrowing heavily before they give up.

Second, these investments are unwise because the only way someone can purchase good quality property with no money down is if deception is involved. To get a lender to finance one hundred percent of a property, somebody probably lied about the property's value.

Let me give an example. Suppose that I were going to buy some property for $50,000, but I wanted one hundred percent financing. So I asked the seller to mark it up to $75,000 and to indicate to the bank that I had $25,000 cash invested. It would appear to the lender that I had invested a third of the property's value when in reality I hadn't. Unfortunately, this has been done often.

I would avoid no-money-down real estate investing. Look for properties with good value and discipline yourself to save the money necessary for a reasonable down payment. As Proverbs 1:10 says, "My son, if sinners entice you, do not consent."

Question 21:

I'm a Christian in full-time ministry. Over the years I think I have been approached with every multilevel product sales scheme that exists. I question the validity of Christians recruiting each other to be salesmen and distributors, with all the hype and the promise of big money. Do you agree?

I think we first have to differentiate between pyramid selling and multilevel sales. In the former, an individual buys the right to bring somebody into an organization, and he receives a commission or finder's fee. In other words, no product is sold, only a "franchise." With rare exception, this system is illegal because the franchise is considered a security and is governed by the individual state's security laws. Those who get involved normally are not licensed securities dealers.

In multilevel sales, several people in a marketing chain make a percentage on the sales of those below them. Multilevel selling is a widely accepted marketing system.

In fact, virtually every product sold in America is multilevel. The manufacturer produces a product and marks it up to the wholesaler. The wholesaler marks it up to the retailer. The retailer marks it up and sells it to the consumer.

The difference in the multilevel selling you presented is that a participant not only makes a percentage of sales but also has the right to earn commissions on sales of people he brings into the business. All of this is legitimate, provided that the product is good quality, and the intent is to sell a product and not just recruit more sales people.

The difficulty in multilevel sales is the attitude of those who get involved. Sometimes greed and materialism take over.

If Christians want to engage in this activity, I believe some fundamental principles should be observed: 1) They should care more about other people than themselves. I have had Christians who were involved in this ask for a list of my counselees with financial problems so that they could "help" them. The pitch was, "We can get them into our product line, and they can make all the money they need." I suspect the real motive was to profit from them. 2) Christians must be sure that their sales techniques are honest. Some products and companies are so deceptive in their approach that people get suspicious of any "opportunity" in multilevel sales. 3) Don't proselytize in your church, Bible study, or other Christian network. These people are brothers and sisters in the Lord, not sales prospects. Any time a product has to be sold exclusively within Christian circles, I get suspicious, doubly so if a minister is involved. It's too easy to abuse a pastoral relationship this way. As Paul said in 1 Timothy 6:9, "But those who want to get rich fall into temptation and a snare and many foolish and harmful desires which plunge men into ruin and destruction."

Question 22:

I work at a casino in Las Vegas where I have been for several years. I have recently become a born-again believer, and now I have a conflict about gambling. Is it wrong?

Gambling in itself is not prohibited scripturally, as best I can discern. Several instances of gambling or chance are found in the Bible. One reference in the New Testament describes the apostles drawing lots to replace Judas (Acts 1:26).

"But that's not really gambling," you say.

It certainly was, only the stakes were not monetary. God judges motives, and the motive for modern gambling is to get rich quick.

Proverbs 21:5 says, "The plans of the diligent lead surely to advantage, but everyone who is hasty comes surely to poverty." In other words, when you hasten to get rich fast, you can get poor even quicker.

It's not the gambling itself that's wrong. It's the attitude about it. Gambling caters to many people's weaknesses and can easily become addictive.

The vast majority of gambling is done by those who can least afford to lose the money. The average gambler's income is about $11,000 a year, so it's clear that gambling preys on the poor.

For a Christian, gambling is a bad witness, and to participate lends credibility to those who promote it. However, ultimately you must decide if working in a casino is a compromise of your beliefs.

Question 23:

For the last few years my husband and I have been involved with sweepstakes. We only enter those that offer prizes without requiring money to be put up. We search through magazines and fill out all the forms regularly, and we have begun to win some prizes. But I'm having doubts about what we're doing. Does this constitute gambling, and is it wrong?

Contests such as sweepstakes certainly are a form of gambling.

But it's not the sweepstakes in themselves that are wrong; it's what they promote. They promote a get-rich-quick attitude. They also promote the attitude that gambling is a way to gain without having to work.

Some people can keep it in balance and not overdo it. For them, gambling is a harmless pastime. For others, it destroys their families and finances. For some, gambling is as much an addiction as drinking is to an alcoholic.

Promotions like sweepstakes have helped to legitimize gambling in the minds of an entire generation. Even though you might not be risking money, you're still encouraging a potentially dangerous attitude of trying to get something for nothing.

There are two additional potential dangers with "free" sweepstakes. First, you might pass a get-rich-quick attitude on to your children. Second, your involvement could become a stumbling block to a weaker brother.

God promises that He will prosper His children. I guarantee that He can do so without gambling. "He who tills his land will have plenty of bread, but he who pursues vain things lacks sense" (Prov. 12:11).

CHAPTER 10

Buying and Selling

Have you ever wondered if you really need all that insurance on your home, cars, health, and life? If you don't carry insurance, are you expressing faith or presumption? If God promises to provide all of our needs, does that include replacing a car if it's totalled? Would He want you to leave your family with little or no provision when you die? After all, He does tell us that if He feeds the birds, He can feed us also.

Should I expect Christians who own businesses to give me a better deal because I'm Christian, too? As a businessman, should I give ministries a special discount because they are doing God's work?

Most Christians have asked these questions at one time or another; in this chapter on buying and selling, we'll look at the answers.

Question 1:

Do you believe that a business should offer special discounts to ministries and churches?

No, I don't. I believe that when you have a differing price structure, it's the equivalent of what Scripture refers to as having differing weights in your bag. Proverbs 20:23 says, "Differing weights are an abomination to the Lord, and a false scale is not good." Obviously, when you give a discount to someone, the intent is not to cheat someone else, but that's how it's perceived. Unless you're willing to tell everyone that you give a special discount to Christian groups, then it's deceptive.

I suggest, rather than giving discounts, that you charge a fair price and then make a donation equivalent to the discount. A gift is totally your option, and nobody will feel overcharged.

Question 2:

What if you're shopping for second-hand merchandise to resell in business, as my husband and I do, and you come across an item that is greatly underpriced? Should you buy it at that price and consider it good business, or should you tell the person that it's underpriced and pay what's fair for the product?

That question is very pertinent to our generation. Some time back, I read a newspaper article about a man who, while browsing at a rock sale, saw what he immediately recognized as an uncut ruby. He bought it for $10; it turned out to be worth more than $3 million. The papers publicized this find as a "shrewd" deal from a smart buyer.

But there's a very thin line between shrewdness and deceit. Sometimes deceit doesn't mean telling a lie, just not telling the entire truth. Suppose the seller were unsaved, and the buyer were a Christian. What kind of a testimony would he or she have?

Everything we do should glorify the Lord. Someone else's ignorance doesn't relieve our obligation to put others first. "Do nothing from selfishness, or empty conceit, but with humility of mind let each of you regard one another as more important than himself" (Phil. 2:3).

The example of a $3 million profit makes the principle clear. But the percentage of profit is not the issue; the heart attitude is. God provides us with opportunities to reach the unsaved. Don't let the world rob you of them just for the sake of gain. As the Apostle Paul said, ". . .Do not be conformed to this world, but be transformed by the renewing of your mind" (Rom. 12:2).

Question 3:

We just had our first child, and we've been looking at life insurance policies and their costs. I wonder, does buying life insurance show a lack of faith?

Obviously the Bible doesn't speak directly about life insurance, but it does address provision for a family. In Ecclesiastes 6:3, Solomon wrote, "If a man fathers a hundred children and lives many years, however many they be, but his soul is not satisfied with good things, and he does not even have a proper burial, then I say, 'Better the miscarriage than he.' " Clearly the father is responsible to provide for his family through his labor, but even if he dies prematurely, he still must provide.

In the past his sons took over his business or land and provided for the family. If he had no son, his closest male heir assumed that responsibility. Today, I believe that insurance is a substitute means of providing for our families should a man die prematurely.

I would suggest you use insurance to provide, not to protect or profit. It should only replace the income that would be missing if you died. As you accumulate more assets, your need for insurance should decline.

I don't believe insurance necessarily represents a lack of faith in God's provision. It may be wise planning, as described in Proverbs 24:3.

Question 4:

How can I determine what my actual life insurance needs are?

Three questions need to be answered to determine your life insurance needs. First, how much insurance is needed? A simple rule of thumb is to calculate the annual income your family would need if you died.

For instance, if you make $25,000 per year, and Social Security would provide $10,000 per year, there would be a shortfall of $15,000. Multiply that amount times ten, and you have the approximate amount of insurance needed to replace your income. In other words, $150,000 worth of insurance invested at ten percent would provide the $15,000 your family would need. Add to that other one-time expenses, such as college education, mortgage retirement, etc.

Once you know how much insurance you need, the second question is, How much can you afford? The answer to this question is in your budget.

Let's assume again a $25,000 per year salary with a net spendable income of approximately $20,000. About five percent of that total, or approximately $1,000 a year, could be spent on life insurance.

The third question is, What kind of insurance should you buy? The answer is to buy the insurance that provides the amount needed at a price you can afford. For most young couples who need the maximum coverage when they have the least money, this is an inexpensive term insurance plan.

Question 5:

We're a couple in our mid-twenties. We're just beginning to have a family and are looking for life insurance. Can you tell us the best kind of life insurance for our family?

There is no "best" kind of insurance. That's a little like walking into a doctor's office and asking, "What's your best operation?" The type of life insurance that's best for your family depends on your specific needs. Two basic types of insurance are available: term and whole life.

"Term insurance" means insurance that is purchased for a determinable period of time. Annual renewable term is purchased for one year and must be renewed each year. Ten-year term must be renewed after ten years, etc.

Whole-life means that the policy is in force for your whole life. Whole-life is also known as cash-value insurance because it accumulates a cash reserve. Generally, I recommend term insurance for most young couples with limited income because of its low cost and because the family needs maximum coverage when the children are young.

The most common argument against term insurance is that you only rent your insurance, you never own it. I find that a shallow argument, because most people don't accumulate cash reserves in their automobile or health insurance either.

Conversely, the argument against cash value insurance is that you can beat the savings if you buy term and invest the difference in a good mutual fund. But, in reality, few people actually follow through on their intent to do this.

Each family must decide which plan best fits its needs. No single plan fits everyone, and every agent thinks his or her plan is the best.

Question 6:

Is it necessary to have life insurance on my wife and children? I am the primary wage earner, and I have adequate insurance on myself.

There are two logical reasons to have insurance on your wife. One is for burial expenses. The other is to provide extra funds to care for the children, if necessary. The amount of insurance on the wife would normally be substantially less than that on the husband.

In my opinion, I don't believe insurance for children is necessary except to cover the cost of burial. An argument often made for insurance on children is to guarantee their insurability in later years. However, only a small fraction of people are uninsurable at the time they marry; therefore, I believe the potential risk does not justify the cost of buying insurance at a young age.

Question 7:

We've been shopping for insurance and looking at the various plans, both term and cash-value. There are so many products available that it's difficult to understand them. A friend told me that the cash accumulation in an insurance policy belongs to the company and not to the policyholder. Could you clarify this?

In reality, your friend is right. The cash values in an insurance policy do not belong to the insured or to the beneficiaries; they belong to the insurance company. The cash is accumulated to offset a portion of the company's liability. Let me use an example.

If you bought an annual renewable term policy, each year when you renewed the policy, the costs would go up. The obvious reason is that your life expectancy is less the older you are, so the company's risk is greater. The same principle applies to whole life or cash-value insurance. The difference is that they start off charging a higher premium at the younger age and place a part of the overcharge in reserve: the cash value. The cash reserve builds over the years and helps to offset the increased risk. When you die, the cash values go to the insurance company.

For example, say you bought a $100,000 policy at twenty years of age, and at fifty your policy has $50,000 worth of cash value. If you died, your beneficiaries would not receive the face value of the insurance, $100,000, plus the cash value of $50,000. They would receive only $100,000. So the actual out-of-pocket expense to the insurance company is $50,000, not $100,000. Accumulated dividends may also be in the policy. These dividends do belong to the insured and the beneficiaries.

Most insurance companies also offer the option of borrowing the cash value. If you borrow against the cash value and die before the loan is repaid, your insurance will be reduced by the outstanding loan.

Question 8:

We want to buy life insurance, and we would also like to make an investment. Some insurance policies pay interest on the cash in the policy. The rates look competitive with other types of investments. What do you think?

First, let me say that I'm not an insurance specialist. So my evaluation of insurance is generally non-technical. Myriads of policies are available that pay dividends, interest, paid up insurance, etc. Some require a lump-sum payment in the beginning, others require a minimum payment plan for five to seven years, and still others require payments for your entire life. It's virtually impossible to comment on any one plan without reviewing and comparing it. But, in general, you need to verify the actual return on invested dollars.

Although an insurance plan may promise a rate from seven to ten percent, its guaranteed rate may be as low as three to four percent. Many policies quote their rates in gross earnings, but in reality the actual interest paid to the policyholder may be two to three percent lower than that because of administrative charges and commissions.

So you need to compare the net earnings in an insurance plan to the net return from a good quality mutual fund. In general, I have found that a good quality mutual fund will return more than an insurance plan.

Question 9:

My wife and I are looking to put money aside in a retirement plan. An insurance agent in our church recommended that we buy an annuity. I'm not familiar with annuities. Could you help us?

An annuity is basically an insurance policy for future income. You pay into an annuity for a given number of years, and it pays you a monthly income at a predetermined age.

For example, a thirty-five-year-old man who pays into an annuity for thirty years to retire at, say, sixty-five-years-old. He contributes $100 a month to the annuity for thirty years, and the annuity guarantees him $1,500 a month in income for the rest of his life, beginning at age sixty-five.

Two types of annuities exist: fixed and variable. The annuity I described above is a fixed annuity, meaning it will pay out a fixed amount of money per month. A variable annuity means that the payout varies, depending on the earnings of the company.

For employees of nonprofit organizations, there is an additional type of annuity available: a tax-sheltered annuity (TSA). The money put into a TSA is exempt from Federal, State and FICA taxes until payout. But a TSA is only available to employees of nonprofit organizations under the IRS code 501.

Question 10:

Do you believe that a Christian should have health insurance?

This is a great expense to us, as we are not part of a group insurance plan. Is having health insurance a lack of trust?

God created us to live in a physical world in which there are things beyond our control, such as accidents and diseases. The treatment for these can cost hundreds of thousands of dollars. With the exception of those people who are under conviction not to have any form of insurance, health insurance is a reasonable and logical expenditure.

If you are not part of a group health insurance plan, I recommend a major medical insurance policy. A major medical plan has a high deductible (perhaps $1,000 or more), so it provides for catastrophic medical expenses only.

Health insurance rates vary significantly from company to company. If you're in a low-risk group, such as non-smokers and non-drinkers, you may qualify for health insurance with other low-risk people. These are called trust groups.

For further information, one of the best insurance resources is an independent Christian agent.

Question 11:

We just moved into our first home and purchased a fire insurance policy through our mortgage insurance company. We've since learned that we could have purchased a homeowner's policy with better coverage for less money. Could you tell us what options are available in homeowner's insurance policies?

A homeowner's insurance policy is a comprehensive insurance plan covering the home, its contents, and any liability associated with the property. Usually, a homeowner's policy is the least expensive way to insure a dwelling.

When we bought our first home, we also bought a fire insurance policy through the mortgage company. At the time, I didn't know any better either, and they sure didn't tell me. Later I found that I could have bought a homeowner's policy for about half of what I paid.

For renters, there is a renter's policy. It is similar to a home-owner's policy except that the renter's version covers the home's contents and liability, but not the dwelling.

Remember that the key to buying good insurance is to provide, not to protect or profit. If you can afford a higher deductible, then you're going to get a better rate.

Question 12:

I have a disability insurance policy that costs nearly $300 per month. I know that's expensive, but as a commercial pilot, I could lose my pilot's license for any number of health reasons. Do you have reasonable alternatives or helpful counsel?

Disability insurance for anyone is going to be relatively expen-sive. As an airline pilot, you probably need some kind of disability or license insurance. But you don't need one that will pay you for the rest of your life. I would suggest a policy that will provide a transition period, perhaps two to five years. That would allow you time to get the retraining necessary to earn a living in another area.

As Christians, we need to accept that God can redirect us. David said in Psalm 37:25, "I have been young, and now I am old; yet I have not seen the righteous forsaken, or his descendants beg-ging bread."

Question 13:

We're ready to buy our first home, and we've been trying to decide between a new or used house. There are advantages either way, and we can't decide which is best. Can you give us some guidelines?

The advantages to buying a new home are: 1) you can design the home to fit your own particular needs; 2) you can locate it where you want it to be; and 3) you can usually get better financing on a new home.

The disadvantages of a new home are: 1) With few exceptions, those who build a new home end up spending more than they planned. If you have never built a home before, there are always alterations you'll make as the house goes up. It's the "in work" changes that cost a lot of money. 2) It takes considerable time and effort (mental) to oversee the construction of a new house. Virtually every new home buyer will tell you that you must check almost every day or things will happen that you don't like.

The advantages to buying a used home are: 1) you know exactly what it's going to cost, because you can settle on a single price; and 2) you can get more extras with a used home. Usually, it has curtains, curtain rods, towel racks, lights in the closets, light bulbs, an established lawn, shrubbery, etc. Those things help to make a house a home.

The disadvantages of a used home are: 1) if you have to secure a new mortgage, fewer mortgage companies want to refinance an older home; 2) you're not going to be able to relocate it; and 3) in general, you're going to have to take it as is. Anytime a house has been lived in, it will have some wear and tear; the older the home, the more things that need repair. If the house is ten years old or more, you should check the heating and air conditioning system, the roof, and the hot water heater.

Personally, I believe it's better to buy an existing home if it's your first, for two reasons. You don't need to bother with overseeing the construction, and you know exactly what your costs are.

Question 14:

We have the opportunity to refinance our house at a lower interest rate than the existing loan we have. Would it be better for us to refinance for a shorter term and maintain the same payments? Or to go for the longer term and lower our monthly payments? Also, how can I determine whether it's better to refinance, or whether the cost of refinancing will be more than the reduced interest rate?

Generally, the number of years you finance your home depends on your budget. If you have been able to manage the payments within your budget and can reduce your payment period from thirty years down to fifteen, I would recommend that. I also recommend that, as you have additional funds available, you use them to accelerate your mortgage even faster.

To determine if it's economically advantageous to refinance, you need to find out the total closing costs and discount points on the new loan. Then compare those costs to what you will save in total interest by refinancing.

Question 15:

We're an older couple approaching our retirement years. Our home was paid off approximately five years ago, but it's much larger than we need. We've been thinking about selling it and using the equity to purchase a manufactured home and investing the difference for additional income. Do you have any counsel?

Obviously, manufactured housing to most people in our country is called a "house trailer." That has such a bad connotation that many people avoid even considering it. However, I have known many couples who have purchased new manufactured homes and thought they were great. It gave them better housing than they could have afforded otherwise and satisfied the needs of their families for many years. A great many older couples who retire go into manufactured housing and live very well.

The major disadvantage with manufactured housing is the depreciation. A new mobile home will lose about twenty-five percent of its total value when it leaves the sales lot.

If you don't expect to live in your mobile home for the rest of your life, I would suggest a previously owned one, because someone else has already taken the depreciation.

Question 16:

We need to buy an automobile, but we haven't saved enough

cash. Is it better for us to buy a new or a used car? Can't we get better financing on a new car?

The enticement of low-cost financing tempts many young couples into buying a new car. But remember, you don't get something for nothing. The dealer may offer a low interest loan on a new car, but you'll probably pay more for the car.

Whether you should buy a new or used car is best answered by the car's use. If you drive 40,000 to 50,000 miles a year, it's probably better to buy a new car, or at least a demonstrator. However, if you drive considerably less than that, a used car is usually better. The depreciation on a new car is approximately twenty-five percent the day you drive it out of the showroom.

Question 17:

We're interested in buying a car. We will probably buy a used car, but we don't have enough money to pay cash for it. Since we're going to have to borrow, could you tell us how to find the lowest interest rate?

When you're going to finance an automobile, there is really no best way. However, there are different methods of calculating the interest. Always ask the lender to quote the rate to you in annualized percentage rate (APR). Then you can compare the cost of one against another. If you can use assets other than the automobile as collateral (stocks, bonds, etc.), often you can negotiate a lower interest rate. But I encourage you not to use the equity in your home as collateral. Many couples who do this end up creating a ten- or fifteen-year note for an automobile. The automobile will be worn out long before the note wears out.

Question 18:

Do you believe that Christians should carry insurance on cars? Should we carry comprehensive and collision insurance? What about uninsured motorists?

Most states' laws require you to carry liability insurance on your car. Even if your state does not require it, I recommend that you carry liability because the risk is great and the cost is relatively small. One "at fault" accident can put you in debt for the rest of your life. Proverbs 22:3 says, "The prudent sees the evil and hides himself, but the naive go on, and are punished for it." So be prudent.

The question about carrying collision insurance depends on whether you can afford to "self-insure." For instance, if your car is worth $2,000, and you maintain $2,000 in a savings account, you probably don't need collision insurance. Also, when you consider the value of an older car, the cost of collision insurance can be disproportionately high.

Comprehensive insurance covers miscellaneous damages, such as a broken windshield or the theft of articles from your car. Generally, the cost is low for the coverage provided.

Regarding uninsured motorist insurance, I recommend that you carry it. Although most state laws require liability insurance, many drivers have no insurance (or license). These are often the most accident-prone drivers.

Question 19:

My wife and I have been living on your budget plan for the last year. We are rapidly paying off all of our indebtedness, but how will we ever buy things like new furniture? Your budget has no percentage for furniture, appliances, etc.

The budget plan we've discussed (see the chapter on budgeting) is a short-term budget. It's designed to cover a one-year period and as such does not include long-term purchases such as furniture or appliances.

For most families, those purchases will be made out of what I call "windfall profit," meaning funds that come in beyond your regular budget. If the budget is adhered to, then raises, overtime, bonuses, gifts, etc. become the "windfall" you can use for larger items.

The first portion of your windfall should go to the Lord as a tithe. The second portion goes to the government as taxes. Then, the remainder can be used for irregular purchases, such as furniture.

CHAPTER 11

Vocational Decisions

Question 1: Is it possible to find the right vocation?

Question 2: Should I quit if I don't like my job?

Question 3: Should Christians only work for other Christians?

Question 4: Are some vocations unsuitable for Christians?

Question 5: Should women plan careers?

Question 6: Should I stay with a job that pays poorly?

Question 7: Should a wife earn more than her husband?

Question 8: What if the husband is called to the mission field but his wife isn't?

Nearly half of all working Americans say they are dissatisfied with their vocations. But they also feel that they can't afford to change careers. Why do so many people get trapped into jobs they don't enjoy or have a heart for? Because of two fundamental problems: first, an almost total lack of vocational planning in our society; and second, the affluence of our high-pressure generation that forces young people to take on too much debt too soon.

A large part of God's plan for our lives is that we have fulfillment through how we earn a living. Too often today the work environment is the least enjoyable part of life. Many Christians suffer through thirty to forty years of job dissatisfaction just waiting for retirement. That is not God's plan for His people.

I don't know that we're supposed to leap out of bed every morning, shouting, "Praise the Lord, I get to go to work today!" But if Friday at 5 p.m. is the best part of your week, and Monday at 8 a.m. is the worst, you can't be in God's will vocationally.

Your work is a part of your witness, but if you don't enjoy it, you won't be likely to do it well. "Do you see a man skilled in his work? He will stand before kings; he will not stand before obscure men" (Prov. 22:29).

This section should help to answer most of the common questions about making vocational decisions for adults and children.

Question 1:

I've tried several different career fields since college, but I've yet to find one that I enjoy. I question if I even know what I want anymore. Can you give me some guidance?

I don't know that God has the "perfect" vocation for anyone. But until you find the career field that fits your abilities and personality, you'll never be happy. At this point, it's apparent that you have not found that career field.

It's important to narrow down a career field as early in life as possible, even if you can't decide on a specific job. Obviously, everyone is going to be different. One person will make a good salesman, the next a good accountant, while another may make a good administrator. It's important to recognize the differences and help to match your abilities to a specific career field.

Too often people get trapped into the wrong career because of life-styles. I believe that's why so few Americans, Christians included, are satisfied with their jobs. If you're committed to serving God through your vocation, find the job that gives you the most peace and fulfillment. Don't make your decisions based on pay or esteem. As Proverbs 15:16 says, "Better is a little with the fear of the Lord, than great treasure and turmoil with it."

Question 2:

I have been on the same job for more than fifteen years, but I don't really like it, and I never have. I'm a driver for a package delivery system, and it's all I know how to do. Should I change jobs?

I certainly can't answer that question for you. You and your wife should pray about this together and seek God's direction. But if you're tied to a job that you dread, you cannot be in God's will.

If you'll turn this area of your life over to God, one of two things should happen. He will either give you a peace about staying where you are, or move you to where you should be. "And everything you ask in prayer, believing, you shall receive" (Matt. 21:22).

Question 3:

Should Christians only work in Christian career fields or jobs, such as ministry, Christian schools, Christian music, etc.?

Absolutely not! God has placed Christians in every segment of society and career field, all the way from the President of the United States to a janitor at a public high school. We each have a different area of ministry.

Christians should not seek out Christian jobs, unless they feel that's God's plan for their lives. God has called us to be salt and light, and there's no way you're going to shed light into darkness unless you go where the darkness is. So God will have Christians in every career field in every community of the world.

Question 4:

Do you believe there are any vocations that are not suitable for a Christian?

Most assuredly there are. The obvious ones are those that involve anything illegal, immoral, or unethical. That covers vocations all the way from drug dealing to abortions. If you're referring to working in a gambling casino or liquor store, that decision must be based on your conviction as a Christian. The same can be said of a hotel manager where the parent company allows pornographic movies. These can represent a compromise to God's Word and a stumbling block to others. I would encourage you to seek the counsel of mature Christians in your area and to pray diligently. "Listen to counsel and accept discipline, that you may be wise the rest of your days" (Prov. 19:20).

Question 5:

Isn't it true that the majority of women who are educated and trained in a career field never work in it? If most women are going to become housewives and mothers, why should we waste the money on our daughter's college education?

It's true that many women don't stay in their chosen career field during childbearing years. But with more working women than in the past, many are establishing continuing careers. I wouldn't discount your daughter's education. It can be applied in her own family when she has children, and it will be useful to her later when the children are grown.

You need to view your daughter's education as an investment

and not feel that it is a waste. Just be certain that she has specific goals that require a college education.

The real waste is to spend four years in college to avoid making a career decision. "Give instruction to a wise man [or daughter], and he [she] will be still wiser, teach a righteous man, and he will increase his learning" (Prov. 9:9).

Question 6:

What should I do if I have a job that I really like, but it doesn't pay enough to meet my family's basic needs?

Unfortunately, your situation is not unusual, especially for those in Christian education. Most Christian school teachers thoroughly love what they do, but they simply don't make enough to meet their families' needs.

My counsel is two-fold. First, see if God provides your family's needs from another source. It may be gifts from others, an inheritance, or some other windfall. If your needs are provided, then the decision to stay or go is a matter of choice. But if your needs are not provided, then you must look elsewhere, even though you enjoy your work.

This issue of paying inadequate salaries, especially within Christian school ministries, is one that must be confronted. Eventually the best, most qualified people must move on to jobs that provide their needs. Then Christian education is going to be staffed with underpaid, underqualified people. If we can buy buses and buildings, we can certainly pay a fair day's wage. "But if any one does not provide for his own, and especially for those of his household, he has denied the faith, and is worse than an unbeliever" (1 Tim. 5:8).

Question 7:

I'm a working wife with no children. My salary is almost twice that of my husband's. Although we both know that we need the money, he resents that I make more than he does. Should I quit or take a lesser job? Is it his attitude that needs to change?

I have counseled with several couples where the wife made more money than her husband, and it's a rare husband who is able to handle it. It's easy to say, "That's his problem."

But, in fact, God placed the leadership of a home on the husband. He should want to be the provider for his family. "You husbands likewise, live with your wives in an understanding way, as with a weaker vessel, since she is a woman" (1 Peter 3:7a).

If you find that you're unable to reach an amenable agreement about your income, then you need to pray about seeking another job. I know it seems that you need the money, but that's always true, no matter how much or how little you make. The question is, what's more important in your life, the relationship with your husband, or the material things that the additional money can provide?

Question 8:

What should a husband do if he feels called by God to be a missionary, but his wife and children resent the idea of living in a foreign country? Should I do it anyway?

I find it very difficult to believe that God would call a husband to the mission field without also calling his wife. That may be an indicator that you aren't one spiritually.

If your wife is unsaved, I would not recommend the mission field for you. It's difficult enough when you're both totally committed to the sacrifices you will face.

If she is a Christian but remains opposed to mission work, you need to seek counsel as a couple. Ultimately, the decision is yours. But since your wife is one-half of you, listen to her counsel and weigh it heavily. Ask your Christian friends and your pastor to be totally honest about what they see. It could be that your wife is simply vocalizing what others feel, too.

CHAPTER 12

Singles' Finances

177

Question 19: Who pays the debts when a couple divorces?

Question 20: How can I establish credit as a newly divorced woman?

Question 21: How do I handle delinquent taxes my former husband is responsible for?

Question 22: What can I do about fraudulent tax returns my husband and I filed when married?

Question 23: How do I pay back a church that helped during my divorce?

Question 24: How can our church help needy divorced women?

Question 25: Loving divorced people without judgment.

Singles are the rule, not the exception, in the church today. When singles, divorcés, divorcées, widows, and widowers are combined, they comprise as much as forty percent of the average church congregation.

Single parents, divorced and widowed, account for up to thirty percent of most urban churches. They have the greatest financial needs of any group of Christians in our generation. The average divorcée with dependent children is twenty-eight years old, with an income of $13,000. The average widow is fifty-two years old, with few assets and very little work experience.

In this chapter, we will deal with many of the questions asked by singles. I would hope that those Christians who are not widowed or divorced will also read through these few pages and gain a better appreciation of the plight of single parents in the church today.

Question 1:

I'm a recent college graduate, thinking about getting married. However, I owe about $12,000 in school debts and my fiancé owes about $10,000. Together, we would have to pay out more than six hundred dollars a month, just on those debts. Could you give us some counsel?

I suspect at this point you both understand the principle taught in Proverbs 22:7: "The rich rules over the poor, and the borrower becomes the lender's slave."

You probably can't afford to get married just yet. I recommend that you and your fiancé concentrate on retiring some of those debts first. Only after you have them down to a percentage that will fit a married couple's budget should you consider getting married. Your debt payments, excluding home and automobile, should not exceed eight percent of your net spendable income. If they do, your budget won't balance. Remember that half of all marriages in America fail, and eighty percent of those that fail were having financial problems. So don't start out with a heavy debt load.

Question 2:

I'm a single woman almost thirty years old. I believe that God wants me to get married, although I've not met the right person yet. I'm living with another woman, who has no concept of managing money. When it comes time to pay our utilities and rent, she never has enough money. I would like to help her, but I don't really understand how to budget. Could you give me a budget that will work for a single person?

Yes, a budget for a single is not significantly different from that of a couple. The percentages in a few categories are different. For instance, if you live with someone and share the rent and utilities, your housing allowance is probably thirty to thirty-five percent of your net spendable income, or about the same as a married couple. But if you move out on your own, your percentage for housing could easily double. Food is another category that changes with singles since eating out is a big part of the single life-style. So their food budget drops, but entertainment and recreation increases. Other categories, such as medical, dental, clothing, miscellaneous, savings, etc., aren't going to change significantly.

I would suggest that you view your budget as a whole. In other words, if it balances by reducing one category and increasing another, that's fine. But be certain that you allocate for non-monthly expenses like annual insurance premiums, vacations, clothing, etc.

I would further recommend that you use the envelope budget system. That means for categories such as entertainment and recreation, spending money, and miscellaneous, you put the budgeted amounts in envelopes. Then, when you entertain or recreate, pay for it out of the entertainment envelope and put the change back in. When you look into your entertainment and recreation envelope and it's empty, you stop entertaining and recreating until you get paid again. Practice spending based on the budgeted amount, not on what is in your checking account.

Question 3:

I live at home with my parents at their request. I've tried many times to give them money to help with expenses, but they say they just don't need it. If my parents want me to live with them and not pay any rent or living expense, do you think it's all right for me to do so?

There's nothing wrong with a young single person living at home with his or her parents. However, to have some degree of autonomy, I would suggest that even if your parents don't want you to help financially, that you do so anyway. If they won't take the money, set up an account in their name at your bank. I believe this will accomplish two things: 1) It will help you establish the discipline of paying your way. 2) It will demonstrate to your parents that you are an adult.

Obviously, if you live in their home, you're still under your parents' authority. But at some point, you're going to have to make a transition to establish your own life. If they don't need the money later, they can always make a gift of it back to help you buy a home. "A man who loves wisdom makes his father glad. . ." (Prov. 29:3a).

Question 4:

I'm a recent widow in my mid-forties with three children. The only funds I have available are in my husband's life insurance. Also, I receive Social Security benefits as long as I have dependent children at home. My question is: What is the best way to handle the life insurance proceeds? The insurance company has offered me two options. One is to receive the proceeds in cash as a lump sum, and the other is to receive an annuity that would pay me for the rest of my life. Do you have any counsel about which is better?

In general, I would say that you will be better off taking the annuity, with a guaranteed income. I would weigh the annuity's income against other very secure investments, such as CDs or government securities.

If, however, you elect to receive the payment in cash, let me give you some cautions. The first is to put the money into an insured savings account for at least one year. I would suggest either government bonds or a savings account insured by the FDIC.

The second is to make no long-range financial decisions during the first year. Under no circumstances turn over your finances to anyone to invest for you until you are thoroughly recovered emotionally. I can't stress how important this is. Many widows make hasty decisions the first year, including buying new homes, new cars, and risky investments based on bad counsel. Relax the first year and deposit your money safely, even though it may not earn the maximum interest.

No matter what your decision about the insurance proceeds, you need to take time to acquire the knowledge that you need. Talk to financial advisors during that year, but don't do anything hasty. As Proverbs says, "The mind of the prudent acquires knowledge, and the ear of the wise seeks knowledge" (18:15).

Question 5:

I'm a widow in my mid-sixties. My husband left me an adequate amount of insurance and other assets so I can live comfortably. But I was wondering if I should take a portion of the money to pay off the mortgage on my home. I have a six percent mortgage, and a counselor from my local church tells me that I should be able to earn at least twenty percent on my investments. Do you have any advice?

Anything can happen in our economy, and any investment can be lost. And let me assure you that regardless of what happens in the economy, a mortgage will survive, because it's the lenders who are protected by law. My counsel would always be to take a portion of your assets to retire your home mortgage. I realize that many financial counselors would disagree, but that doesn't change my advice. I have counseled many people who never thought they would lose their wealth, but they did when the economy turned down. Any investment, whether it is a farm, oil and gas, precious metals, art, or anything else, can fail when the economy sours.

I would suggest you do what Proverbs 19:20-21 says, "Listen to counsel and accept discipline, that you may be wise the rest of your days. Many are the plans in a man's heart, but the counsel of the Lord, it will stand." In other words, take your counsel from the Lord. As a widow, He is your primary counselor. If you have peace about paying off your home, do it. If you don't have peace about paying it off, don't do it.

Question 6:

My husband died approximately a year-and-one-half ago and left me his sales company. The company did very well when my husband was alive and is still very profitable. The manager we had running the company is still running it and would now like to buy it. Would I be better off selling the business to our manager or keeping it?

First, you need to get some business people from your church to help you evaluate what to do. You also need to get good, independent counsel to evaluate the business' worth.

Normally, I would counsel a widow not to immediately sell her husband's business if she has the ability to run it herself. But if you weren't involved in the business on a day-to-day basis, it's probably better to sell it. Again, I'd recommend that you gather a support group of Christian business people from your church to help you evaluate this decision.

Here's one caution: If you wait too long to sell a sales-oriented business, a key employee might start his or her own company, using your customer base.

However, a word of encouragement from God's Word will help to balance any fears about your business' future. In Psalm 14:9, the Word says, "The Lord protects the strangers; He supports the fatherless and the widow; but He thwarts the way of the wicked." I would turn to God and claim that promise, because God knows exactly what your needs are, and He can intercede to protect your interests.

Question 7:

I am a widow living off a trust fund set up by my husband. Our children are grown and have no need for funds at this point. I've met a widower my age and am considering getting married, but he has been living on a disability pension. Without my income, it would be difficult for us financially. The trust prescribes that it can only be used for my personal support and can't be used to support a future husband. It lasts for my lifetime, and then the principal goes on to my children. How can I go into this marriage knowing that my income can only be used for my personal support?

I suggest that you be totally honest with your future husband, telling him exactly what the terms of the trust are. If you can't live off his income, he needs to know that you must maintain separate accounts.

At this point, you have three alternatives: 1) Disclaim any interest in the trust and learn to live off his income. 2) Get married and keep your personal finances separated, so that you're obeying the intent of your husband's request. 3) Remain single and assume that this relationship is not God's plan for your life.

Obviously, I don't know the answer. But I believe that as you pray about it, God will give you both guidance about what you're supposed to do.

Question 8:

I'm a widow in my late fifties. When my children were at home, I received Social Security benefits, but now they're all adults and the Social Security benefits have ceased. Presently I am living off the proceeds of my husband's life insurance, which is barely enough to get by. When I retire, can I qualify for Social Security, even though I have personally never worked and never paid into the system?

According to the Social Security Department, you can qualify under your husband's Social Security death benefits. But the amount you will draw is less than he would have been able to draw at retirement.

I recommend that you contact your local Social Security Administration Department and verify the benefits you will qualify for. Be sure to apply by age sixty-one, because it may take from nine to twelve months to get qualified.

Question 9:

I'm a widow in my late thirties with five children. My husband was killed in an airplane crash, and the insurance settlement from the airlines was approximately $500,000. My husband was also a government employee, and that settlement was approximately $200,000. After I tithe and put away the money for our children's education, I will still have nearly $500,000 to invest. Over the past few weeks I have been inundated with people trying to help me invest this money. I just don't know whom I can trust.

You do need counsel, but you need to take some time before making any financial decisions. I recommend that you go to your pastor, acquaint him with your situation, and ask him to help you put together an accountability group from your local church to act as advisors to you, but with no vested interest. In other words, they should have no interest in selling you a product, services, or anything else.

As a widow, you need good, unbiased counsel from a group of men and women that can help you weigh your alternatives. "Without consultation, plans are frustrated, but with many counselors they succeed" (Prov. 15:22).

Question 10:

I'm a widow with three children, one in college, a seventeen-year-old who will go to college next year, and a thirteen-year-old. We're living very comfortably on the proceeds of the insurance left by my husband, as well as the assets that we had accumulated before his death three years ago.

I want to thank you for your counsel about making no long-term decisions the first year or two as a widow. I'm going into my fourth year and now have a sound investment plan and my home is paid off.

But I have a question. My car is approximately seven years old. It has more than 100,000 miles on it, and I'm beginning to wonder if I can trust it. Do you think it would be all right for me to buy a new car? I don't plan to buy an expensive one. I know that you normally recommend used cars, but I don't know enough about a car to determine a good one from a bad one.

First, you need to evaluate the kind of a car you need. Then, go to some independent sources and verify the most reliable models. I personally use *Consumer's Report* magazine. Your local library should have a copy.

Whether to buy a new or a used car is really personal preference. There is nothing wrong with buying a new car if you can afford it and it suits your needs. However, if your only hesitation in buying a used car is how to evaluate it, I recommend that you locate someone in your church who can help you. If you ask around, I'm sure someone would be glad to help. If you decide to buy a used car, perhaps a demonstrator would better meet your needs. Much of the depreciation on a demonstrator has already been absorbed by the dealer, and the car has been driven long enough to verify that it doesn't have any major defects.

Question 11:

I'm a fifty-eight-year-old widow, and the last of my children just graduated from college. I no longer need the size home that I now have. I've thought about selling it and buying a condominium to free me from the problems of repairs, maintenance, and yard work. Do you have any counsel?

In Luke 14, the Lord asks, "Would a man consider building a tower without considering its entire cost?" So I would advise you, if you're going to sell your home and buy a condominium, to consider the entire cost. You'll have some expenses getting your home ready to sell, as well as some selling costs like termite bond, sales commissions, title search, etc.

When you buy a condominium, even if you pay cash, there is usually a monthly maintenance fee. Depending on the condominium complex, this fee can range from $50 a month to as much as several hundred dollars a month.

If you don't like yard work and house repairs and can afford the monthly fees, a condominium may suit you well. I'd suggest that you visit condominium complexes and talk to some of the tenants. Most of them will be glad to share their experiences. It might be a good idea to rent your home for a year and lease a condominium, just to be sure you will like it.

As Proverbs 13:10 says, "Through presumptions comes nothing but strife, but with those who receive counsel is wisdom."

Question 12:

My husband died about a year ago; now, for the first time, I'm in charge of everything financial. When my husband was alive, he took care of our budget, paid the bills, and gave me the money I needed for groceries and living expenses. Over the last year, through some rather bad experiences, I found out that I can handle my money better than most financial "experts." I'm far more cautious than they are. But now, my oldest son (early thirties) would like to go into a business, and he's asked if I would lend him about $50,000. I actually have about $200,000 total. Do you have any counsel that would help?

I don't know your son, but I would say that sounds like too much of your assets to risk. Never lend (to anyone) more than you're willing and able to writeoff.

If your son wants to start a legitimate business, there's nothing wrong with helping him. However, I would say that lending $50,000 to anyone to start a first business is too high a risk for a widow. You could probably afford to risk $15,000 to $20,000 and still have enough left to live on. But certainly not $50,000.

I would suggest two things. First, tell your son that you can't lend $50,000, but that you could lend a lesser amount, provided he would be willing to submit himself to the counsel of older, godly men from your church.

Second, go to your pastor and ask him to bring together an accountability group to meet with your son, evaluate the business, and provide continuing accountability. You will be doing yourself and your son a favor. "For by wise guidance you will wage war, and in abundance of counselors there is victory" (Prov. 24:6).

Question 13:

My husband divorced me approximately two years ago. Obviously, there were many reasons for the divorce, and I take a part of that blame. But that's not my issue. I'm committed to pray for my husband, and I'm trusting that God will restore our marriage one day.

But my husband is not supporting us as the divorce decree requires. He provides only a portion of what he promised per month, and there are some months when he doesn't pay anything. Some friends in our church have recommended that I sue him for nonsupport and lock him up if he doesn't support us. Could you give me some counsel?

It would be very easy to tell you to take your husband to court and lock him up if he doesn't support his family, because that's the way I feel about it. I believe he has failed in his responsibility and is worse than an "infidel" (ref. 1 Tim. 5:8). However, I must give the counsel that I believe our Lord would give if you asked Him. The only way to do that is to go back to the source of truth, the Bible.

In Ephesians 5:22, the Apostle Paul wrote, "Wives, be subject to your own husbands, as to the Lord." The argument may be made that he's no longer your husband. But he really is. God does not recognize divorce, and until such time as your husband remarries or dies, he is still your husband in God's eyes. In the same passage, husbands are commanded to love their wives. The point could be made that he is not loving you, so you don't need to honor him. But it's not a bilateral commandment, it's a unilateral commandment. It doesn't say, "Wives, be subject if your husband loves you," but simply, "Wives, be subject" and "Husbands, love your wives."

In Colossians 3:18, the same admonition is given. The real issue is if you're willing to obey your husband. Even a slave is asked to obey his master in this passage. Then, in verse 24, the Apostle Paul tells us if we do as God asks, He fulfills His promise. "Knowing that from the Lord you will receive the reward of the inheritance. It is the Lord Christ whom you serve." Your husband may never come to the Lord or repent of his error. That's his decision. But the certainty is, he will never be able to say it was because of you, and I believe God will honor you.

I also recommend that you do everything biblically possible to get him to support his family. Write him letters, see him personally, phone him, even have the deacons from your church confront him face to face. But I would counsel you not to sue your husband.

The obvious question then becomes, what if he doesn't fulfill his commitment no matter what you do? Then it's your right to present your needs before your church and ask the congregation to help support you. It's their responsibility from that point on.

Question 14:

My husband of thirty-five years recently divorced me and married a younger woman. He was a successful businessman who ended up in great financial difficulty over the last few years. Although I thought we had a positive marriage, apparently he didn't, because he came in one afternoon and said that he no longer loved me and had met somebody else that he wanted to marry. I've learned to handle it now, but where do I go from here? At one time, I was a fairly skilled secretary, but I have not worked in thirty years. Who will hire a fifty-three-year-old ex-secretary?

The first help is from God's Word. I recommend that you read Psalm 50:14-15 and meditate on it. It says, "Offer to God a sacrifice of thanksgiving, and pay your vows to the Most High; and call upon Me in the day of trouble; I shall rescue you, and you will honor Me." God is capable of providing your every need, including healing emotions and finding you a job.

I also recommend, as I always do, that you go to your pastor, present this need, and ask the church to help. Somewhere within your church family a business needs your skills, ability, and loyalty. You may have to hone your skills by going back to school for a few months, but approach the church about helping financially so that you can get re-employed. Later you can repay the church so that they can help others.

By word of encouragement, I have counseled many divorcées who were in similar situations. None of them starved, all of them found productive jobs, and many saw the Lord intercede miraculously.

Divorce is never pleasant; in fact, it's a trauma for everybody involved, and God hates it. But just because you're divorced, don't feel that God has abandoned you. He still knows what your needs are, and He is going to meet them. Just keep a positive attitude and know that God goes before you. "Therefore do not be anxious for tomorrow; for tomorrow will care for itself. Each day has enough trouble of its own" (Matt. 6:34).

Question 15:

My situation is not much different from many women today. My husband of twenty-five years came in one day and told me that he was leaving. He said he could no longer stand the pressure, that we had had no relationship for a long time—which is essentially true—and he left. He provided me with a sizeable amount of money, perhaps enough to live on for the rest of my life if I conserve it carefully.

I feel like I need to get productive and get back into life. I know that my husband and I aren't going to get back together, since he remarried almost immediately. I've accepted it, but I believe that God still has a plan for my life. I'm willing to get the education or the training that I need. My question is: How do I go about finding a new career at fifty years old?

You must decide what you want to do. If you could have your heart's desire, what would you do to be productive? One of the first things I would recommend is that you take an inventory of who you are and what you would like to do for the rest of your life.

Let me use as an example a woman that I counseled several years ago who was in a similar situation. Her husband divorced her and married another woman. She was also nearly fifty years old. She had sufficient money to live on, but she knew that she had to get active, because the divorce had literally destroyed her confidence. Although she was a college graduate, she had never worked outside her home.

After reviewing her alternatives, she decided that she needed to go back to school to get a graduate degree. In graduate school, she took a class dealing with learning-disabled children. She was so intrigued by this area that she began to research and found very few teachers were skilled in the area of learning disabilities. So she decided to concentrate her studies there. She attended every class available, as well as every seminar and conference on the subject. After completing graduate school, she returned home and approached the school board about working as a volunteer with children with learning disabilities.

She did so well that the school board later funded her position. She is now the director of learning disability education, involving hundreds of children. She is known as an authority on learning disabilities and speaks at conferences throughout the country. Her age was not a handicap, nor was her lack of experience and skill.

When she let go and began to trust God, she found that He still had a plan for her life. "I have been young, and now I am old; yet I have not seen the righteous forsaken, or his descendants begging bread" (Ps. 37:25).

Question 16:

One of my greatest expenses as a divorcée is child care. I get very little support from my husband, so I have to work just to meet even our basic needs. Child care consumes nearly half of my take-home pay. At this point, I don't really know what to do. I would like to stay home with my children, but it's impossible. Do you have any suggestions?

I wish I could say "go to your local church, present this need, and they will help." But unfortunately, that's not the way it is. The church doesn't know what to do with divorcées. They're treated rather like lepers were at one time. We feel sorry for them. We would like to help them, but we don't want to get too close to them.

But my counsel is still to go to your church, present your needs, and ask for help. You must be willing to submit yourself to the church's authority, which may require that you receive financial and spiritual counseling. That way the church can be assured funds are being used properly and that you are willing to restore the marriage if possible.

You have the right to expect your church to meet this need. Unless God's people, particularly single parents, are willing to take their needs back to the local church, it will never change. "But whoever has the world's goods, and beholds his brother in need and closes his heart against him, how does the love of God abide in him?" (1 John 3:17).

Question 17:

Several months ago, my husband told me that he no longer wanted to be married to me. I found out that he had been seeing another woman for quite a long while, and their intent is to get married as soon as we're divorced. I've tried everything I can to stall, delay, and avoid this divorce, but it seems irreconcilable. My husband has offered me a cash settlement. Would it be better to take a lump sum or a monthly payment?

It's difficult to give good counsel in a bad situation. However, if your husband is determined to go through with the divorce, my advice is to take the cash settlement. At least that guarantees the income to you and your children.

Under any circumstance, divorce is very difficult. It's much like a death in the family, only worse, because it doesn't seem to end. Don't do anything hasty or impulsive with your money. Wait a year before making any major decisions.

I appreciate your comment about not being able to alter the circumstances of your divorce. I have often heard people say, "It takes two to get a divorce." But in reality, it doesn't always take two. If a husband decides to go, there is basically nothing a wife can do, and vice versa.

I had a close friend whose wife left him after nearly twenty-five years of marriage. It devastated him. He is a well-known Christian counselor, and for a long time he felt the divorce was a reflection of his faith. Later his ex-wife told him that she never did accept Christ, and it was his faith that irritated her.

Question 18:

Ever since my divorce, my children and I have really been struggling to make ends meet. Their father supports the children, but only modestly. He sometimes works, but most of the time does not. I find that I just don't earn enough to make it on a month-in and month-out basis. Do you have any advice?

First, you need to get financial counseling to be sure that you're properly handling the funds you have. Then, if you need help, you should go to your church and present your needs. This is difficult and embarrassing, and most people would rather not do it, which is precisely why the church does not accept this responsibility anymore.

Isn't it amazing that most Christians feel the liberty to stand up in church and ask others to pray about an illness, but don't feel they have the right to stand up and ask for financial help? Satan has duped us into believing that money is his domain. God's plan is found in 2 Corinthians 8:14: "At this present time your abundance being a supply for their want, that their abundance also may become a supply for your want, that there may be equality."

Question 19:

I'm a recent divorcée with financial problems. We were separated off and on for the last three years, and permanently separated for the last year. My husband remarried immediately and left the state. We ran up some indebtedness when we were together, and I know that I'm partially responsible. I have committed to pay at least half of the debts. But while we were separated the last year, my husband charged several thousand dollars on his credit cards. Now creditors are coming after me. They are threatening to garnish my wages and take me to court if I don't sign for the indebtedness. Could you give me some advice please?

First, I would say you probably need a good, Christian attorney. See if an attorney in your local church can help you. Second, don't sign anything until you get legal counsel. I would also encourage you to locate a financial counselor who can help work out a settlement with these creditors. Obviously, some of the indebtedness was encountered while you and your husband were together and is your responsibility. You should begin to pay on that. However, the indebtedness incurred by your husband while you were separated clearly is not your responsibility; it's his. Usually once the creditors understand the circumstances, they will back off. You will probably need someone to intercede on your behalf, so the creditors will know you're telling the truth.

I would encourage you to do what you can and not to worry about what you can't do. Don't take on guilt because of your husband's deceit. As Proverbs 11:3 says, "The integrity of the upright will guide them, but the falseness of the treacherous will destroy them."

Question 20:

After nearly twenty years of marriage, my husband left me for another woman. I'm trying to locate a job and get re-established, but I don't have any credit history. I can't even buy a car. Can you tell me how to establish credit as a single woman?

First, be very cautious about establishing credit. If you're not careful, it can get you into a great deal of trouble, particularly during this transition period of your life.

In answer to your question, you can qualify for credit using your payment history while you were married. Obviously, the extent of the credit will be based on your current income, so until you find employment you would not qualify.

Let me also encourage you to take your financial needs to the Christians around you rather than incur debts you may not be able to handle. Once you have stabilized your income, then re-establish your credit.

Question 21:

I've been divorced for about two years. When we were married, my husband never filed our taxes on time. Now I find that he didn't file taxes at all for the last two years. I didn't work while we were married, but we did file a joint tax return. So even though we're divorced, the Internal Revenue Service says that I owe delinquent taxes, and they are going to foreclose on my home. My question is: Am I responsible for the taxes my husband didn't pay, even though I didn't have an income?

I presented this issue to an attorney, and his opinion is, for the years when you filed a joint return, you are legally responsible for the taxes. He felt that since you didn't generate any income, if you would go to your district IRS office and discuss the matter with them, they would most probably pursue your husband and not you. He also recommended that you contact a good Christian CPA or tax attorney in your area and have that person go with you. You

will not be liable at all for the years when your husband failed to
file a tax return.

Question 22:

*I'm a divorcée. When we were married, my husband and I both
worked. He was a tax protester, and for several years we filed
fraudulent tax returns, not declaring the proper amount of income.
Now I'm a Christian, and I feel that I must confess and make restitution. But if I do so, the IRS will pursue my ex-husband as well as
me. My tax attorney says that since I'm voluntarily turning myself
in, they probably won't prosecute me. But my husband is clearly
guilty of fraud, and they might prosecute him. Would this be a wife
going against her husband?*

Each of us is individually responsible to God, wives included.
If you were turning your husband in and you weren't a participant,
the answer would be more clouded. In this case, if God has convicted you to confess and make restitution, that's exactly what you
should do. If, as a consequence of your confession, your husband
gets caught up in his own web, then so be it.

I would recommend before you go to the Internal Revenue Service, that you contact your husband and let him know what you are
going to do. At least give him the opportunity to confess and offer
restitution at the same time. As the Lord said in Matthew 5:25-26,
"Make friends quickly with your opponent at law while you are
with him on the way; in order that your opponent may not deliver
you to the judge, and the judge to the officer, and you be thrown
into prison. Truly, I say to you, you shall not come out of there,
until you have paid up the last cent." I believe you're doing the
right thing. I trust that your husband will, too.

Question 23:

*I'm a divorcée that's been helped greatly by my church. My
husband had been a deacon in the church, but he got caught up in*

an adulterous affair. Instead of repenting, he became callous and even sued our pastor for removing him as a deacon. After the divorce, the church recognized that I had financial needs because my husband would not support us, so it has helped us every month for the last three years. I now have a job that provides all of my needs and an abundance above that. I'm going to give to my church so that it can help others, but what else would you suggest?

I would suggest to any divorcée, get involved in the lives of those who are less fortunate than you. It will help to refocus yourself outward instead of inward.

For example: many of the elderly people in our churches are virtually abandoned. Single parents, like yourself, can have a great ministry helping the elderly, perhaps just having them over to your home where they can encourage and counsel your children. Another area of ministry can be with young families who have children and need some free time but can't afford baby-sitters.

Romans 13:8 says, "Owe nothing to anyone except to love one another; for he who loves his neighbor has fulfilled the law." This Scripture literally means, do not be left owing. In other words, do more for others than they can do for you. It's this attitude that develops love within the body of Christ.

Question 24:

Some time past, our church got involved with a financial counseling and benevolence ministry for single parents. One of the major problems is that many of the divorcées, particularly those middle-aged, simply don't have the skills to compete in our society. How can we as a church help meet those needs?

Two points need to be made. First, some of these women should not be out working. They should be able to stay home with their children, if necessary. The church should consider them as they would any other ministry and provide their needs until such time as the children are in school. I know that's a major undertaking and shouldn't be taken lightly, but collectively it is possible. What an influence the church could have in the lives of single parents if it would grasp this opportunity. The government has attempted to do this and has failed abysmally, because it can only provide the physical needs. Only God's Word can provide the spiritual needs.

Second, I would encourage you to begin an education program. The first part would be to train single parents in how to handle their finances properly. After all, most divorces start with financial problems. The second, and simultaneous, part would be to train them to understand and follow God's Word in every area of their lives.

The third part, then, is to establish skill-related classes, such as English and secretarial skills. If you don't have the facilities or the people to do that, then I would recommend that you contact a good technical vocational school and work out a cooperative plan.

Many helps can be provided, and it's time that God's people got active in meeting the needs of those within our churches. "And the King will answer and say to them, 'Truly I say to you, to the extent that you did it to one of these brothers of Mine, even the least of them, you did it to Me' " (Matt. 25:40).

Question 25:

Some time back, we as a church began a benevolence ministry for divorced parents. One of the difficulties we found is that many Christians have a judgmental attitude toward those who have gone through divorce. It would seem in Christianity that you would be better off murdering your spouse than suffering through a divorce. We will offer the pulpit to a repentant murderer, but won't reach out a hand to a repentant divorced person. God's Word teaches that we are to love without being judgmental. I clearly understand the principle of not condoning or supporting divorce, and we don't as a church. I teach against divorce, and I teach the alternatives to divorce. I also teach that those who are divorced should remain single as long as their spouses are not remarried. We do every-thing possible to discourage divorce. But, if a divorced person within our congregation is seeking help and is willing to conform to our established rules, then we try to help without judging.

Divorce is no greater sin than any other sin. Divorce is running rampant in our society today, and we certainly don't want to con-done it. But we must learn to hate the sin and love the sinner. Sim-ply ignoring the problem does not seem to have curbed the divorce rate at all. So perhaps we need to go the other way. By caring for the needs of divorced parents and helping them with child care, clothes, food, or housing, perhaps we can bring real Christianity into their lives, and then God can change the multiple divorce rate.

Amen, and thank you.

CHAPTER 13

Retirement

In this section we will discuss how to plan for retirement, including examining retirement plans—IRAs, pension plans, annuities, etc. But even more fundamental than how to plan for retirement is the question, Why retire?

Retirement, as we know it, is a new concept. It really took hold in the fifties when companies began to offer retirement incentives as a part of labor contracts. Retirement is a by-product of the great affluence that allows us to live longer and healthier. Also, there have been plenty of younger people to fill the employment vacancies. Over the last several decades, virtually all Americans, including Christians, have oriented their lives toward retirement at age sixty-five or younger.

But is retirement a scriptural principle? Should God's people store funds for retirement when hungry people abound worldwide? Are there scriptural guidelines that would justify investing for twenty, thirty or even forty years in the future?

What about those who are unable to set aside retirement funds during the working years? Is there a retirement plan that works for them, too? What if someone is approaching age sixty but has no retirement plan; is there anything he or she can do? These questions and others will be discussed in this section on retirement.

Question 1:

I'm in my early thirties, married, and have two children. So I guess I'm one of the average Americans. My company allows me to invest five percent of my salary in a retirement plan, and it matches the funds. I know it's a good deal, and we can afford it, but is retirement scriptural? If not, how did we get so caught up in it?

There is only one reference to retirement in the Bible: Numbers 8:25. It says the priests of the tent meeting (later the Temple) should retire from that function at fifty years old.

So apparently retirement was not common to God's people, including in New Testament times. It can be said that people didn't live as long back then, which is generally true. But they did live long well into Abraham's day, and yet retirement wasn't mentioned.

To put it in the right balance, it would seem clear that, biblically speaking, God's norm is for us to stay active all of our years. So at best, retirement should be a transition to a different vocation, but not a lapse into non-productivity.

Most people obviously can't do the same work at sixty-five as they did at twenty-five or forty-five, but they can do something. Retirement planning, then, should involve financial planning to supplement earnings in later years and vocational planning for life at sixty-five, seventy-five, and even eighty-five.

Those who do no planning during the high income years (years of harvest) may find the senior years (winter) very lean. Proverbs 6:6-8 says, "Go to the ant, O sluggard, observe her ways and be wise, which, having no chief, officer or ruler, prepares her food in the summer, and gathers her provision in the harvest."

Question 2:

I'm self-employed and don't have any retirement plan. Would an IRA be the best way for me to save toward retirement? How should the funds be invested?

An IRA is a good supplemental retirement plan. But unless you start at a young age, the yearly contribution restriction of two thousand dollars (presently) limits its effectiveness. It's certainly better than doing nothing, but because you're self-employed, you have access to a more flexible plan: the HR-10 or Keogh plan.

The HR-10 retirement plan allows contributions up to fifteen percent of your income, or seven thousand dollars per year. Even though you may not be able financially to contribute the maximum amount at a younger age, this flexibility will be very useful from about age fifty on.

You can select from a wide range of investments for either an IRA or Keogh, provided that you invest with a management company that allows you to "self-direct" the use of the funds. Most banks now also offer that option. I would recommend investing in a good quality mutual fund that offers several different investment programs for retirement funds.

Remember that your long-range retirement goals should include not only the minimum amount you feel is necessary, but also the maximum. Once you have reached your pre-established goal—that's enough. Luke 12:20 says, "But God said to him, 'You fool! This very night your soul is required of you; and now who will own what you have prepared?' "

Question 3:

I'm in my mid-fifties and can free about one hundred dollars a month to put toward retirement. Would I be better off to invest it in an IRA or use it to accelerate my home mortgage? I also have a good company retirement plan that will provide half of my salary when I retire.

Assuming that you have adequate savings for current budget needs, I would always recommend paying off the mortgage. Eliminating your mortgage and then using the funds you were paying each month to invest seems a lot more logical. That way you own your home, no matter what, and your retirement income needs decrease by the amount of your payments.

However, if you can't eliminate the mortgage before retirement, and you plan to sell your home after retiring, it may make more sense not to pay off your existing mortgage. If your mortgage is an older fixed rate, assumable loan, it can be a real asset in attracting a potential buyer.

Question 4:

I've worked for a company for thirty-five years; during the last twenty years, it has contributed to an employees' retirement plan. Last year the company filed for bankruptcy protection, and now we find out that our retirement account is also bankrupt. They say they can only pay fifty percent of the promised benefits. I'm scheduled to retire next year, and I can't live on that. I'm hurt, angry, and confused about what to do. Do I have any options; how could this happen? How can a company use employee retirement funds?

It's unfortunate that what you described is all too common today. It's not unusual for a company to borrow funds from its employee retirement account. In many ways, it makes sense because the company gets its capital at a reduced rate, and the retirement account earns a higher rate than it could through a bank deposit. However, too often the loans are unsecured, and the company is a poor risk. If the company fails, the retirement plan fails with it.

It's also unfortunate that only government regulation will prohibit this situation from happening even more often in the future. Others who work for companies with employee retirement accounts would be well advised to get a copy of the annual financial statement and see how much is owed to the retirement plan by the parent company.

In your situation, little can be done except to plan to work longer and pray that your company can survive the bankruptcy.

Question 5:

I have the opportunity to retire at fifty-nine and would like to do so. Could you tell me what the disadvantages of early retirement are?

The first disadvantage has nothing to do with finances. Unless you have specific plans for what you intend to do, retirement can be very traumatic. Many people think they want to retire, but find they miss the friendships and daily routine that work provides. Fifty-nine is certainly too young to become idle (so is seventy-nine, in my opinion), so be sure you have well-defined goals. Be diligent to invest your time productively, and it will multiply, too. As the proverb says, "The hand of the diligent will rule, but the slack hand will be put to forced labor" (Prov. 12:24).

Usually accepting early retirement means accepting reduced retirement benefits in addition to the lost wages you could have earned. If, for instance, your retirement income were reduced by $100 per month, compared to retiring at age sixty-five, and your annual salary was $25,000, your actual loss to age seventy-nine would be approximately $175,000, excluding any income earned after retirement. So this decision should never be taken lightly.

Question 6:

I'm planning to retire in about a year at age sixty-five. I paid into Social Security at a younger age, but I've worked as a schoolteacher for the last thirty-five years and was exempt from Social Security. Can I collect benefits on what I paid in earlier?

The rules for minimum Social Security benefits (FICA) have changed over the years, and your benefits are governed by the rules when you contributed to the system. In general, if you paid in during at least forty quarters when your wages were subject to FICA, then you are entitled to at least the minimum retirement benefits.

Since the percentage of withholding has also changed over the years, your benefits will be based on the years during which you contributed. For instance, if you paid the minimum withholding for the years 1955-1965, your retirement benefits would be approximately $240 per month. If you had paid during 1980-1990, your benefits would be approximately $600 per month. To determine your actual benefits, you need to have your local Social Security Administration office evaluate your records.

Question 7:

I've recently retired from a large corporation and taken my retirement as a lump sum payment. I would like to know where to invest the money safely since it represents the majority of my future income.

I would first refer to the section on investing to get a clear understanding of risk versus return. You need to settle in your mind that, if you seek to gain the highest return of your money, you must accept a high degree of risk. I would recommend a strategy based on preservation of the capital before income. As Will Rogers once said, "I'm not so concerned with the return on my money as I am the return of my money."

One of the best strategies for retirement investing is diversification. As Solomon said in Ecclesiastes 11:2, "Divide your portion to seven, or even to eight, for you do not know what misfortune may occur on the earth."

I suggest that you first develop a budget to determine what your actual needs will be. Invest the amount of retirement funds it takes to provide your budget needs in very secure investments, such as government securities, insured deposits, etc. Once your income is secure, then diversify the remaining funds into good quality mutual funds, first mortgage loans, stocks, precious metals, whatever you feel comfortable with. This will provide a hedge against inflation and can grow for future needs. But don't be coaxed into risking what you can't afford to lose, even by seemingly sure profits. I've seen a lot of "sure things" fail.

Question 8:

I'm a retired pastor who never paid into Social Security. A friend said that, if I would work part-time long enough to qualify for minimum benefits, I could draw Social Security in addition to my pension. I thought that since I elected to be exempt as a pastor I couldn't qualify. What do you think?

As a pastor, you have the option of being exempt from the Social Security tax on wages earned as a pastor. The exemption doesn't apply to wages earned from other sources. Your friend is correct; you can qualify for minimum benefits by paying into the system after retirement for at least forty quarters. This is traditionally called "double-dipping" because many workers, such as federal employees, retire under their system and then qualify for Social

Security benefits. I personally have a problem with the ethics of that, but it is legal.

Question 9:

Both my wife and I are approaching retirement age. Our primary income will be Social Security. With all the publicity about how underfunded the system is, I wonder how secure our Social Security really is. Do you have any information that might help?

The best that anyone can do is offer an opinion on the solvency of the Social Security system. In my opinion, those who are already drawing benefits will be protected to the extent of our government's capability.

The potential difficulties for them are two-fold: First, inflation can easily destroy the value of any fixed income retirement plan. Social Security has a cost-of-living adjustor built into it, but any prolonged inflationary cycle would almost certainly require this to be modified. The government simply lacks the funds to override double digit inflation. Second, the trend in Congress is toward shifting costs such as Medicare to the recipients and taxing benefits at some future date. Either of these can create havoc when you're living on a minimal income.

In your case, since both you and your wife will be drawing retirement benefits, if one of you should die, the survivor may be faced with inadequate income to meet needs. I would encourage you to work at least part-time and develop a savings plan that can eventually provide additional income outside of Social Security.

For younger workers just entering the system, the future of Social Security doesn't look good. We have fewer new workers contributing to the system, and recipients are living longer. Almost certainly, retirement ages will be pushed back and benefits will be reduced beyond the year 2000. In 1935, the system began with seventeen contributors for each recipient. By 1980, it was seven to one, and by the year 2000, it will be four to one. If the trend continues, by 2025 there will be only two contributors for every recipient. In actuality, the system will be bankrupt long before then.

Common sense should tell anyone that an alternate retirement plan would be prudent. As Proverbs says, "The mind of the prudent acquires knowledge, and the ear of the wise seeks knowledge" (18:15).

Question 10:

I teach at a Christian school that has no retirement plan. I contribute to Social Security, but I don't want to depend on that income alone. I have a friend that told me about a Keogh retirement plan. Can I invest in one?

The Keogh or HR-10 retirement plan is exclusively for self-employed people. Normally, as a schoolteacher on salary, you would not qualify from your teaching income. However, if you had income from royalties, honorariums, or other self-employed sources, that income would qualify. The benefits of a Keogh retirement plan are that up to fifteen percent or seven thousand dollars maximum income can be applied toward retirement, and it is tax-deferred (except for FICA or SICA deductions).

If you have no self-employment income, you can still qualify for an Individual Retirement Account (IRA) on income generated by you or your spouse.

Question 11:

I've just started in business and would like to begin a reasonable retirement plan. I don't expect to retire for at least thirty-five years. How much should I put aside and where?

I would suggest that you decide how much income you will need in thirty-five years and work toward that goal. For example, if you retired today, let's say that your income needs would be $30,000 a year. If you could earn an average return of ten percent on your investments, you would need $300,000. If you could maintain your earnings of $30,000 plus inflation, your $300,000 would always meet your goal.

So what you need to do is settle on the current amount needed and save toward that goal in thirty years. Example: if you put aside $17,000 and earned ten percent interest on it (tax-deferred), in thirty years you would have approximately $300,000. You would have to add to the account the annual inflation rate to hold the needed amount constant. If you didn't have the $17,000, you could save approximately $133 a month and still meet the goal.

Saving the funds in a tax-deferred retirement account such as an IRA or HR-10 would be advisable. The actual investments should be selected based on trends in the economy. Normally, no single investment will stay viable over a thirty-year period. At this time, I would personally use a good quality mutual fund that offers diversity.

Question 12:

I was forced into mandatory retirement because of failing eyesight. My retirement income is not sufficient to meet my needs. I can't drive, and I'm sixty years old; who will hire me?

Neither your age (sixty) nor your handicap (sight) are in themselves debilitating. It's only that they don't fit your previous occupation. You need to begin thinking about what you can do, instead of what you can't do. I know of many Christians with similar handicaps (or worse) who are productive and financially self-sufficient.

I would suggest that you seek counsel to evaluate your skills, abilities, and desires. Then look for opportunities to employ your talents. If you require some retraining, let your needs be known in your church and ask for help, as Scripture directs. God knows your needs and will provide them. It's through other believers that He usually does so. As Psalm 34:6 says, "This poor man cried and the Lord heard him; and saved him out of all his troubles."

I've seen God provide for many elderly who were willing and able to use their talents. Some are doing telephone surveys, direct mail marketing, typing, in-home child care, writing, editing, etc.

The list is as long and varied as their individual talents and abilities. Most had never done what they are now doing before retirement. Many are fulfilling a desire they had during their working careers but needed a "push" to get started. Perhaps that's the case with you, too. Remember what Psalm 37:4 says, "Delight yourself in the Lord; and He will give you the desires of your heart."

Question 13:

My husband and I are both retired. I've just retired and have qualified for Medicare, but I've been inundated with offers to buy Medicare supplemental insurance. The costs range from a low of $50 to several hundred dollars a month. Do we need supplemental insurance?

You'll need to weigh the cost of the insurance against the potential liability to evaluate its worth. But, in general, the supplemental insurance protects against catastrophic medical expenses that can wipe out your finances. By the time a Medicare recipient pays the non-reimbursed costs, they can amount to many thousands of dollars. In addition, many doctors are refusing to accept direct Medicare payments because they disagree with the fees Medicare assigns. This makes the patient liable to pay in advance and assume responsibility for the charges above those reimbursed by Medicare. I would recommend a policy that covers all charges above that which Medicare reimburses. The cost may seem high, but not compared to losing all that you have worked for.

Question 14:

I recently retired from the Navy and would like to find a civilian job for the next few years. We've settled in Florida and would like to retire here. My question is, should we buy a home and mortgage it or wait until we can buy for cash? This could be in ten years or so.

As a general rule, I would recommend that, after you settle into a job, go ahead and buy a home, even if you have to use a mortgage to do so. Unless we have a general economic slowdown or depression, homes in Florida probably won't depreciate and, in fact, should increase at a fairly steady rate. I would advise that you accelerate the mortgage payments to retire the debt as rapidly as possible and don't sign surety on the note.

I believe one of the essential foundation blocks of a biblically-oriented financial plan is a debt-free home. This should be the goal of all Christians, but particularly so for retirees.

Anything can happen to this economy, and certainly something will eventually. It may be a depression brought on by a financial collapse or hyper-inflation brought on by printing massive amounts of money to avoid a depression. Either way, you can lose whatever is indebted. A debt-free home is yours, not a lender's.

Personally, I would buy a mobile home if that's what it took to get debt-free at sixty-five or older. If it were necessary to sell a larger home and pare down expenses by buying a smaller debt-free home, I would do that also. We are a nation of debtors, and eventually we will grasp the meaning of Proverbs 22:7, "The rich rules over the poor, and the borrower becomes the lender's slave."

Question 15:

My parents are both retired and in their seventies. They are in good health now, but obviously at their age this could change quickly. They live on Social Security and have a little savings. How can we help them to prepare for the expenses of nursing home care?

You may not appreciate my initial response to your question, but I don't believe God intended for Christians to shuffle their parents off to nursing homes, regardless of what society promotes. There may be exceptions based on unique medical conditions, but we have made the exceptions the rule today. I believe Christians of our generation need to take a refresher course on honoring their fathers and mothers.

The Lord said that we shall reap what we sow; I wonder what will happen to those who commit otherwise normal parents to a life of isolation when they, too, get older.

For those who have medical needs that necessitate nursing home care, only a few alternatives are available. One is an insurance policy for nursing home care. A few companies offer such policies, but the restrictions on age and health are severe, and the costs are very high.

Another alternative is government welfare. Once elderly patients have exhausted all available resources, they usually qualify for state and federal welfare assistance. Let me say here that many otherwise honest Christians have misused this privilege by transferring assets from an elderly relative to other people to qualify for indigent care. This is wrong and to do so willfully is a sin. "But your iniquities have made a separation between you and your God, and your sins have hid His face from you, so that He does not hear" (Isa. 59:2).

Question 16:

I'm retiring at age sixty-two from a large corporation. I took my retirement pay as a lump sum and now need to invest it securely. My yearly income needs are $18,000, and I have $600,000 available. I have two questions: first, should I tithe from my retirement proceeds since I tithed when my salary was earned? Second, where can I invest my money securely so that I don't have to think about it anymore?

First, let me say, there is no place you can just park your money and forget about it. If anyone tells you there is, don't risk a dime of it with that person. The money is God's; your role is to be manager (steward) over it for Him.

I'm not an investment advisor, so the only counsel I can give you is what I would do in your circumstances. You have sufficient capital to meet all of your needs if handled wisely and enough surplus to be able to make more to give away.

First, you need to secure your budgeted income. To earn the $18,000 a year, I would select a government-backed fund. It's best to commit to the longest-term security available, such as a ten-year Treasury bill. The fluctuations in value during the ten years are irrelevant. It's the income from the securities that you're after.

I would take the second part of my assets and speculate a little more by investing in: 1) a good quality mutual fund; 2) good quality first and second mortgages on properties worth at least two to three times the loans; 3) limited partnerships in debt-free income properties such as mini-warehouses, etc.

With the remainder of the assets I would invest in precious metals, mutual funds, growth stock funds, foreign currency funds, etc. This portion of the assets would be used as a hedge against inflation, an economic collapse, etc.

Regarding the tithe, I believe the tithe (that which is returned to God) merely reflects our commitment of the total amount to God. I personally would give even from the return on previously tithed funds, i.e., the retirement funds. A farmer tithes on the increase of his flocks and fields, even though the grain and sheep had been tithed previously.

I believe God's Word teaches that as we acknowledge His total ownership, we can appropriate God's wisdom to manage His wealth. The tithe is nothing more than a reminder that God owns it all. "You shall surely tithe all the produce from what you sow, which comes out of the field every year. And you shall eat in the presence of the Lord your God, at the place where He chooses to establish His name, the tithe of your grain, your new wine, your oil, and the first-born of your herd and your flock, in order that you may learn to fear the Lord your God always" (Deut. 14:22-23). "The fear of the Lord is the beginning of knowledge; fools despise wisdom and instruction" (Prov. 1:7).

Conclusion

I trust that as a result of reading these questions and answers, you've developed a deeper understanding of God's financial principles. In reality, it's not the money that is important; it's our attitude about it.

Money merely reflects to the outside world what's going on inside each of us. For instance, if a husband and wife don't communicate about finances, they don't have a money problem. They have a communication problem that's reflected in their finances.

Most parents think that a sixteen-year-old who leaves jackets and sweaters at school, always leaves the family car cluttered and the gas tank empty, and can't get up on time for any job doesn't appreciate the "value" of things. Actually, it's the lack of parental discipline that's reflected in the child's attitude about things.

This list could go on and on. But it is sufficient to say that quite often what we see materially are the symptoms. What God deals with are the problems, which are usually spiritual. Most of us want relief from the symptoms, and thus we seek a "quick fix." God wants us to be totally free, which requires an attitude change.

It's my hope that a husband or wife who reads this book will make a commitment to go back through it with his or her spouse and discuss the questions and answers together. That parents would review the applicable sections with their children as devotionals. And last, now that each of you is armed with more of God's truth, that you would be able to help others who are floundering from a lack of God's wisdom.

215

People Making A Difference

Family Bookshelf offers the finest in good wholesome Christian literature, written by best-selling authors. All books are recommended by an Advisory Board of distinguished writers and editors.

We are also a vital part of a compassionate outreach called **Bowery Mission Ministries**. Our evangelical mission is devoted to helping the destitute of the inner city.

Our ministries date back more than a century and began by aiding homeless men lost in alcoholism. Now we also offer hope and Gospel strength to homeless, inner-city women and children. Our goal, in fact, is to end homelessness by teaching these deprived people how to be independent with the Lord by their side.

Downtrodden, homeless men are fed and clothed and may enter a discipleship program of one-on-one professional counseling, nutrition therapy and Bible study. This same Christian care is provided at our women and children's shelter.

We also welcome nearly 1,000 underprivileged children each summer at our Mont Lawn Camp located in Pennsylvania's beautiful Poconos. Here, impoverished youngsters enjoy the serenity of nature and an opportunity to receive the teachings of Jesus Christ. We also provide year-round assistance through teen activities, tutoring in reading and writing, Bible study, family counseling, college scholarships and vocational training.

During the spring, fall and winter months, our children's camp becomes a lovely retreat for religious gatherings of up to 200. Excellent accommodations include heated cabins, chapel, country-style meals and recreational facilities. Write to Paradise Lake Retreat Center, Box 252, Bushkill, PA 18324 or call: (717) 588-6067.

Bowery Mission Ministries are supported by voluntary contributions of individuals and bequests. Contributions are tax deductible. Checks should be made payable to Bowery Mission.

**Fully accredited Member
of the Evangelical Council
for Financial Accountability**

Every Monday morning, our ministries staff joins together in prayer. If you have a prayer request for yourself or a loved one, simply write to us.

**Administrative Office:
40 Overlook Drive, Chappaqua,
New York 10514 Telephone: (914) 769-9000**